Nutshell Series

of

WEST PUBLISHING COMPANY

P.O. Box 3526

St. Paul, Minnesota 55165

January, 1983

I

Comparative Legal Traditions, 1982, 402 pages, by Mary Ann Glendon, Professor of Law, Boston College, Michael Wallace Gordon, Professor of Law, University of Florida and Christopher Osakwe, Professor of Law, Tulane University.

Conflicts, 1982, 469 pages, by David D. Siegel, Professor of Law, Albany Law School, Union University.

Constitutional Analysis, 1979, 388 pages, by Jerre S. Williams, Professor of Law Emeritus, University of Texas.

Constitutional Power—Federal and State, 1974, 411 pages, by David E. Engdahl, Professor of Law, University of Puget Sound.

Consumer Law, 2nd Ed., 1981, 418 pages, by David G. Epstein, Professor of Law, University of Texas and Steve H. Nickles, Professor of Law, University of Minnesota.

Contracts, 1975, 307 pages, by Gordon D. Schaber, Dean and Professor of Law, McGeorge School of Law and Claude D. Rohwer, Professor of Law, McGeorge School of Law.

Contract Remedies, 1981, 323 pages, by Jane M. Friedman, Professor of Law, Wayne State University.

Corporations—Law of, 1980, 379 pages, by Robert W. Hamilton, Professor of Law, University of Texas.

Corrections and Prisoners' Rights—Law of, 1976, 353 pages, by Sheldon Krantz, Dean and Professor of Law, University of San Diego.

Criminal Law, 1975, 302 pages, by Arnold H. Loewy, Professor of Law, University of North Carolina.

Criminal Procedure—Constitutional Limitations, 3rd Ed., 1980, 438 pages, by Jerold H. Israel, Professor of Law, University of Michigan and Wayne R. LaFave, Professor of Law, University of Illinois.

Debtor-Creditor Law, 2nd Ed., 1980, 324 pages, by David G. Epstein, Professor of Law, University of Texas.

Historical Introduction to Anglo-American Law, 2nd Ed., 1973, 280 pages, by Frederick G. Kempin, Jr., Professor of Business Law, Wharton School of Finance and Commerce, University of Pennsylvania.

Injunctions, 1974, 264 pages, by John F. Dobbyn, Professor of Law, Villanova University.

Insurance Law, 1981, 281 pages, by John F. Dobbyn, Professor of Law, Villanova University.

International Business Transactions, 1981, 393 pages, by Donald T. Wilson, Professor of Law, Loyola University, Los Angeles.

Judicial Process, 1980, 292 pages, by William L. Reynolds, Professor of Law, University of Maryland.

Jurisdiction, 4th Ed., 1980, 232 pages, by Albert A. Ehrenzweig, Late Professor of Law, University of California, Berkeley, David W. Louisell, Late Professor of Law, University of California, Berkeley and Geoffrey C. Hazard, Jr., Professor of Law, Yale Law School.

Juvenile Courts, 2nd Ed., 1977, 275 pages, by Sanford J. Fox, Professor of Law, Boston College.

Labor Arbitration Law and Practice, 1979, 358 pages, by Dennis R. Nolan, Professor of Law, University of South Carolina.

Labor Law, 1979, 403 pages, by Douglas L. Leslie, Professor of Law, University of Virginia.

Land Use, 1978, 316 pages, by Robert R. Wright, Professor of Law, University of Arkansas, Little Rock and Susan Webber, Professor of Law, University of Arkansas, Little Rock.

Landlord and Tenant Law, 1979, 319 pages, by David S. Hill, Professor of Law, University of Colorado.

Law School: Survival and Beyond, 1983, approximately 300 pages, by Kenny F. Hegland, Professor of Law, University of Arizona.

Law Study and Law Examinations—Introduction to, 1971, 389 pages, by Stanley V. Kinyon, Late Professor of Law, University of Minnesota.

Legal Interviewing and Counseling, 1976, 353 pages, by Thomas L. Shaffer, Professor of Law, Washington and Lee University.

Legal Research, 3rd Ed., 1978, 415 pages, by Morris L. Cohen, Professor of Law and Law Librarian, Yale University.

Legal Writing, 1982, 294 pages, by Dr. Lynn B. Squires, University of Washington School of Law and Marjorie Dick Rombauer, Professor of Law, University of Washington.

Legislative Law and Process, 1975, 279 pages, by Jack Davies, Professor of Law, William Mitchell College of Law.

Local Government Law, 1975, 386 pages, by David J. McCarthy, Jr., Dean and Professor of Law, Georgetown University.

Mass Communications Law, 1977, 431 pages, by Harvey L. Zuckman, Professor of Law, Catholic University and Martin J. Gaynes, Lecturer in Law, Temple University.

Medical Malpractice—The Law of, 1977, 340 pages, by Joseph H. King, Professor of Law, University of Tennessee.

Military Law, 1980, 378 pages, by Charles A. Shanor, Professor of Law, Emory University and Timothy P. Terrell, Professor of Law, Emory University.

Oil and Gas, 1983, approximately 365 pages, by John S. Lowe, Professor of Law, University of Tulsa.

Post-Conviction Remedies, 1978, 360 pages, by Robert Popper, Professor of Law, University of Missouri, Kansas City.

Presidential Power, 1977, 328 pages, by Arthur Selwyn Miller, Professor of Law Emeritus, George Washington University.

Procedure Before Trial, 1972, 258 pages, by Delmar Karlen, Professor of Law, College of William and Mary.

Products Liability, 2nd Ed., 1981, 341 pages, by Dix W. Noel, Late Professor of Law, University of Tennessee and Jerry J. Phillips, Professor of Law, University of Tennessee.

Professional Responsibility, 1980, 399 pages, by Robert H. Aronson, Professor of Law, University of Washington, and Donald T. Weckstein, Professor of Law, University of San Diego.

Personal Property, 1983, approximately 318 pages, by Barlow Burke, Jr., Professor of Law, American University.

Real Estate Finance, 1979, 292 pages, by Jon W. Bruce, Professor of Law, Vanderbilt University.

Real Property, 2nd Ed., 1981, 448 pages, by Roger H. Bernhardt, Professor of Law, Golden Gate University.

Regulated Industries, 1982, 394 pages, by Ernest Gellhorn, Dean and Professor of Law, Case Western Reserve University, and Richard J. Pierce, Professor of Law, Tulane University.

Remedies, 1977, 364 pages, by John F. O'Connell, Professor of Law, Western State University College of Law, Fullerton.

Res Judicata, 1976, 310 pages, by Robert C. Casad, Professor of Law, University of Kansas.

Sales, 2nd Ed., 1981, 370 pages, by John M. Stockton, Professor of Business Law, Wharton School of Finance and Commerce, University of Pennsylvania.

Secured Transactions, 2nd Ed., 1981, 391 pages, by Henry J. Bailey, Professor of Law, Willamette University.

Securities Regulation, 2nd Ed., 1982, 322 pages, by David L. Ratner, Dean and Professor of Law, University of San Francisco.

Sex Discrimination, 1982, 399 pages, by Claire Sherman Thomas, Lecturer, University of Washington, Women's Studies Department.

Titles—The Calculus of Interests, 1968, 277 pages, by Oval A. Phipps, Late Professor of Law, St. Louis University.

Torts—Injuries to Persons and Property, 1977, 434 pages, by Edward J. Kionka, Professor of Law, Southern Illinois University.

Torts—Injuries to Family, Social and Trade Relations, 1979, 358 pages, by Wex S. Malone, Professor of Law Emeritus, Louisiana State University.

Trial Advocacy, 1979, 402 pages, by Paul B. Bergman, Adjunct Professor of Law, University of California, Los Angeles.

Trial and Practice Skills, 1978, 346 pages, by Kenney F. Hegland, Professor of Law, University of Arizona.

Trial, The First—Where Do I Sit? What Do I Say?, 1982, 396 pages, by Steven H. Goldberg, Professor of Law, University of Minnesota.

Unfair Trade Practices, 1982, 444 pages, by Charles R. McManis, Professor of Law, Washington University, St. Louis.

Uniform Commercial Code, 1975, 507 pages, by Bradford Stone, Professor of Law, Detroit College of Law.

Uniform Probate Code, 1978, 425 pages, by Lawrence H. Averill, Jr., Dean and Professor of Law, University of Arkansas, Little Rock.

Welfare Law—Structure and Entitlement, 1979, 455 pages, by Arthur B. LaFrance, Dean and Professor of Law, Lewis and Clark College, Northwestern School of Law.

Wills and Trusts, 1979, 392 pages, by Robert L. Mennell, Professor of Law, Hamline University.

*

Hornbook Series

and

Basic Legal Texts

of

WEST PUBLISHING COMPANY

P.O. Box 3526

St. Paul, Minnesota 55165

January, 1983

Administrative Law, Davis' Text on, 3rd Ed., 1972, 617 pages, by Kenneth Culp Davis, Professor of Law, University of San Diego.

Agency, Seavey's Hornbook on, 1964, 329 pages, by Warren A. Seavey, Late Professor of Law, Harvard University.

Agency and Partnership, Reuschlein & Gregory's Hornbook on the Law of, 1979 with 1981 Pocket Part, 625 pages, by Harold Gill Reuschlein, Professor of Law, St. Mary's University and William A. Gregory, Professor of Law, Southern Illinois University.

Antitrust, Sullivan's Hornbook on the Law of, 1977, 886 pages, by Lawrence A. Sullivan, Professor of Law, University of California, Berkeley.

Common Law Pleading, Koffler and Reppy's Hornbook on, 1969, 663 pages, by Joseph H. Koffler, Professor of Law, New York Law School and Alison Reppy, Late Dean and Professor of Law, New York Law School.

Common Law Pleading, Shipman's Hornbook on, 3rd Ed., 1923, 644 pages, by Henry W. Ballentine, Late Professor of Law, University of California, Berkeley.

Conflict of Laws, Scoles and Hay's Hornbook on, 1982, 1085 pages, by Eugene F. Scoles, Professor of Law,

University of Illinois and Peter Hay, Dean and Professor of Law, University of Illinois.

Constitutional Law, Nowak, Rotunda and Young's Hornbook on, 2nd Ed., 1983, approximately 1000 pages, by John E. Nowak, Professor of Law, University of Illinois, Ronald D. Rotunda, Professor of Law, University of Illinois, and J. Nelson Young, Professor of Law, University of North Carolina.

Contracts, Calamari and Perillo's Hornbook on, 2nd Ed., 1977, 878 pages, by John D. Calamari, Professor of Law, Fordham University and Joseph M. Perillo, Professor of Law, Fordham University.

Contracts, Corbin's One Volume Student Ed., 1952, 1224 pages, by Arthur L. Corbin, Late Professor of Law, Yale University.

Contracts, Simpson's Hornbook on, 2nd Ed., 1965, 510 pages, by Laurence P. Simpson, Late Professor of Law, New York University.

Corporate Taxation, Kahn's Handbook on, 3rd Ed., Student Ed., Soft cover, 1981 with 1982 Supplement, 614 pages, by Douglas A. Kahn, Professor of Law, University of Michigan.

Corporations, Henn's Hornbook on, 3rd Ed., 1983, approximately 1167 pages, by Harry G. Henn, Professor of Law, Cornell University.

Criminal Law, LaFave and Scott's Hornbook on, 1972, 763 pages, by Wayne R. LaFave, Professor of Law, University of Illinois, and Austin Scott, Jr., Late Professor of Law, University of Colorado.

Damages, McCormick's Hornbook on, 1935, 811 pages, by Charles T. McCormick, Late Dean and Professor of Law, University of Texas.

Domestic Relations, Clark's Hornbook on, 1968, 754 pages, by Homer H. Clark, Jr., Professor of Law, University of Colorado.

Environmental Law, Rodgers' Hornbook on, 1977, 956 pages, by William H. Rodgers, Jr., Professor of Law, University of Washington.

Estate and Gift Taxes, Lowndes, Kramer and McCord's Hornbook on, 3rd Ed., 1974, 1099 pages, by Charles L. B. Lowndes, Late Professor of Law, Duke University, Robert Kramer, Professor of Law Emeritus, George Washington University, and John H. McCord, Professor of Law, University of Illinois.

Evidence, Lilly's Introduction to, 1978, 486 pages, by Graham C. Lilly, Professor of Law, University of Virginia.

Evidence, McCormick's Hornbook on, 2nd Ed., 1972 with 1978 Pocket Part, 938 pages, General Editor, Edward W. Cleary, Professor of Law Emeritus, Arizona State University.

Federal Courts, Wright's Hornbook on, 4th Ed., 1983, approximately 775 pages, including Federal Rules Appendix, by Charles Alan Wright, Professor of Law, University of Texas.

Federal Income Taxation of Individuals, 1983, approximately 421 pages, by Daniel Q. Posin, Jr., Professor of Law, Hofstra University.

Future Interest, Simes' Hornbook on, 2nd Ed., 1966, 355 pages, by Lewis M. Simes, Late Professor of Law, University of Michigan.

Income Taxation, Chommie's Hornbook on, 2nd Ed., 1973, 1051 pages, by John C. Chommie, Late Professor of Law, University of Miami.

Insurance, Keeton's Basic Text on, 1971, 712 pages, by Robert E. Keeton, Professor of Law Emeritus, Harvard University.

Labor Law, Gorman's Basic Text on, 1976, 914 pages, by Robert A. Gorman, Professor of Law, University of Pennsylvania.

Law Problems, Ballentine's, 5th Ed., 1975, 767 pages, General Editor, William E. Burby, Professor of Law Emeritus, University of Southern California.

Legal Writing Style, Weihofen's, 2nd Ed., 1980, 332 pages, by Henry Weihofen, Professor of Law Emeritus, University of New Mexico.

Local Government Law, Reynolds' Hornbook on, 1982, 860 pages, by Osborne M. Reynolds, Professor of Law, University of Oklahoma.

New York Practice, Siegel's Hornbook on, 1978, with 1981–82 Pocket Part, 1011 pages, by David D. Siegel, Professor of Law, Albany Law School of Union University.

Oil and Gas, Hemingway's Hornbook on, 2nd Ed., 1983, approximately 507 pages, by Richard W. Hemingway, Professor of Law, University of Oklahoma.

Poor, Law of the, LaFrance, Schroeder, Bennett and Boyd's Hornbook on, 1973, 558 pages, by Arthur B. La-France, Dean and Professor of Law, Lewis and Clark College, Northwestern School of Law, Milton R. Schroeder, Professor of Law, Arizona State University, Robert W. Bennett, Professor of Law, Northwestern University and William E. Boyd, Professor of Law, University of Arizona.

Property, Boyer's Survey of, 3rd Ed., 1981, 766 pages, by Ralph E. Boyer, Professor of Law, University of Miami.

Real Estate Finance Law, Osborne, Nelson and Whitman's Hornbook on, (successor to Hornbook on Mortgages), 1979, 885 pages, by George E. Osborne, Late Professor of Law, Stanford University, Grant S. Nelson, Professor of Law, University of Missouri, Columbia and Dale A. Whitman, Dean and Professor of Law, University of Missouri, Columbia.

Real Property, Burby's Hornbook on, 3rd Ed., 1965, 490 pages, by William E. Burby, Professor of Law Emeritus, University of Southern California.

Real Property, Moynihan's Introduction to, 1962, 254 pages, by Cornelius J. Moynihan, Professor of Law, Suffolk University.

Remedies, Dobb's Hornbook on, 1973, 1067 pages, by Dan B. Dobbs, Professor of Law, University of Arizona.

Sales, Nordstrom's Hornbook on, 1970, 600 pages, by Robert J. Nordstrom, former Professor of Law, Ohio State University.

Secured Transactions under the U.C.C., Henson's Hornbook on, 2nd Ed., 1979, with 1979 Pocket Part, 504 pages, by Ray D. Henson, Professor of Law, University of California, Hastings College of the Law.

Torts, Prosser's Hornbook on, 4th Ed., 1971, 1208 pages, by William L. Prosser, Late Dean and Professor of Law, University of California, Berkeley.

Trial Advocacy, Jeans' Handbook on, Student Ed., Soft cover, 1975, by James W. Jeans, Professor of Law, University of Missouri, Kansas City.

Trusts, Bogert's Hornbook on, 5th Ed., 1973, 726 pages, by George G. Bogert, Late Professor of Law, University of Chicago and George T. Bogert, Attorney, Chicago, Illinois.

Urban Planning and Land Development Control, Hagman's Hornbook on, 1971, 706 pages, by Donald G. Hagman, Late Professor of Law, University of California, Los Angeles.

Uniform Commercial Code, White and Summers' Hornbook on, 2nd Ed., 1980, 1250 pages, by James J. White, Professor of Law, University of Michigan and Robert S. Summers, Professor of Law, Cornell University.

Wills, Atkinson's Hornbook on, 2nd Ed., 1953, 975 pages, by Thomas E. Atkinson, Late Professor of Law, New York University.

Advisory Board

CIVIL PROCEDURE
IN A NUTSHELL

By

MARY KAY KANE

Professor of Law, University of California,
Hastings College of the Law

ST. PAUL, MINN.
WEST PUBLISHING CO.
1979

COPYRIGHT © 1979 By WEST PUBLISHING CO.

Printed in the United States of America

Library of Congress Cataloging in Publication Data
Kane, Mary Kay.
    Civil procedure in a nutshell.
    (Nutshell series)
    Includes index.
    1. Civil procedure—United States. I. Title.
KF8841.K36   347'.73'5   79–11278
ISBN 0–8299–2040–4

Kane—Civ.Proc.
3rd Reprint—1983

To John and Frances Kane, to whom I owe much, much more.

*

PREFACE

This Nutshell is designed to provide the reader with an introduction to and a compact overview of the field of civil procedure. That task may appear at first blush too large for so small a volume. Thus, a few disclaimers are warranted.

Necessarily I have not engaged in an in depth analysis of the many important issues and controversies present in modern day civil litigation. In many places questions are raised and conflicting points of view are mentioned without attempting to answer or resolve them. There is a minimum of citation, primarily to cases that are recognized trend-setters, as this book is not meant to be used for research purposes. In most instances the federal rules are used as the model for how a given issue is treated. Although comparison with different approaches taken by some state courts may be interesting, it was impossible to be exhaustive in this respect. Since the federal rules now have been adopted by so many states as their procedural guidelines, the study of the federal approach seemed to be most reasonable.

A firm understanding of any procedural system, of the issues that face the courts, and of the underlying policies that motivate or suggest certain

solutions should provide an attorney with sufficient knowledge and sensitivity to questions and
problems to be able to adapt easily to the particular rules prevailing in whatever system he or she
is litigating. It is my hope that this volume may
aid the reader in reaching that plateau.

MARY KAY KANE

San Francisco, California
March, 1979

OUTLINE

I. INTRODUCTION

II. CHOOSING THE PROPER COURT

OUTLINE

IV. ADJUDICATION WITHOUT TRIAL

V. THE TRIAL

OUTLINE

VI. JUDGMENTS AND THEIR EFFECTS

VII. APPEALS

VIII. SPECIALIZED MULTI–PARTY—MULTI-CLAIM PROCEEDINGS

OUTLINE

IX.   OTHER SPECIAL PROBLEMS IN
FEDERAL LITIGATION

TABLE OF CASES

References are to Pages

TABLE OF CASES

TABLE OF CASES

*

TABLE OF STATUTES

UNITED STATES

UNITED STATES CONSTITUTION

UNITED STATES CODE ANNOTATED

15 U.S.C.A.—Commerce and Trade

TABLE OF STATUTES

TABLE OF STATUTES

TABLE OF RULES

TABLE OF RULES

FEDERAL RULES OF CIVIL PROCEDURE—Cont'd

TABLE OF RULES

FEDERAL RULES OF CIVIL PROCEDURE—Cont'd

FEDERAL RULES OF EVIDENCE

*

CIVIL PROCEDURE IN A NUTSHELL

I. INTRODUCTION

§ 1–1. General Background

The basic first year civil procedure course is designed to teach how lawyers choose a proper court and how they frame and present their cases throughout the proceedings until a judgment has been reached and all available appeals have been pursued. The impact of judgments on future litigation also may be explored. Thus, the primary focus in this book is on the methods and tools available to the litigator. This study requires an inquiry into both judicially developed doctrines, as well as various rules and statutes governing the civil courts. At times it will produce questions that are theoretical or constitutional; at other times issues of narrow or strict rule interpretation will be paramount. Throughout, it is

[1]

important to keep in mind the purpose for which the rules or doctrine have been developed—to provide a just, efficient, and economical means by which persons can resolve their disputes. Not always will this purpose be met and, as we will see, some of the existing procedures have been used by attorneys to thwart this goal. Nonetheless, the desire to achieve justice, efficiency, and economy in our civil dispute resolution process underlies the way in which the courts apply and interpret the governing rules.

In studying the procedures by which legal rights are vindicated, it also is important to remember that the Anglo-American judicial system is based on the adversary model. The judge sits solely to rule on disputed questions, as presented by the parties, and to apply sanctions when they are properly requested by a party. The lawyers shape the contours of the action. Issues not raised, objections not made, or points not challenged are, with very few exceptions, waived. The case moves forward only in response to the demands of the parties. While modern judges have tended to take a somewhat more active role in guiding litigation before them, it still remains true that the ultimate responsibility for each case rests with the litigants.

Finally, it should be noted that there is a very important aspect to framing litigation that typically is not taught in the basic civil procedure course and will not be discussed in this book: how to select a particular remedy as the one most likely to succeed or best suited to the needs of the client. That inquiry concerns whether injunctive relief or damages may be sought or whether some form of restitutionary relief might be most appropriate. Historically, the question of what type of relief was involved also dictated in which court suit should be filed, as there were separate courts established—i. e., law, equity, ecclesiastical—to dispense certain types of relief or to hear certain types of disputes. Modern court systems are not so designed. Instead, any civil court is authorized to dispense whatever remedy is appropriate. Thus, the problem of framing a remedy, while an essential step in preparing your case, is not particularly relevant in the selection of a court and is left to a course in remedies. An excellent treatment of that problem may be found in D. Dobbs, *Remedies* (1974).

§ 1-2. Current Structure of Court Systems

There are fifty-two separate court systems in the United States. Each state, as well as the District of Columbia, has its own fully developed, independent system of courts and there is a separate federal court system. The federal courts are not superior to the state courts; they simply are an independent system authorized by the United States Constitution, Art. III, § 2, to handle matters of particular federal interest. The presence of two parallel court systems often raises questions concerning the relationship of the state and federal systems, presenting important issues of federalism. See §§ 9–2—9–4, infra. The United States Supreme Court, composed of nine justices, sits as the final and controlling voice over all these systems.

Although a few states have a two-tiered system, most states, as well as the federal courts, are based on a three-tiered model. That means that for any litigant there will be the opportunity to plead his case before a trial court and then, should he lose, there are two levels of appeal at which he ultimately may succeed. For example, in the federal system the trial court is the district court, of which there is at least one in every state. There are eighty-eight districts in the United States and each has one judge or more commonly two or more. After an adverse judgment in the district court, a litigant may appeal to a United States Court of Appeals. There are eleven intermediate appellate courts in the federal system. Each has four or more judges who sit in panels of three to review district court decisions as well as some decisions of administrative agencies. Ultimately a losing litigant may be able to appeal to the Supreme Court. Cases in the state courts similarly may proceed through a trial court, a state appellate court, and then the state supreme court. If a federal constitutional question is involved the decision of the state supreme court may be appealed to the United States Supreme Court.

Three-tiered systems vary on the role which the highest court plays. The approaches taken reflect differing philosophies with regard to what the highest court should do. For example, in California only criminal cases in which capital punishment has been imposed are appealable as of right to the state supreme court. Appeals as of right to the United States Supreme Court are limited to federal constitutional questions. An appeal will lie only when a federal appellate court has held a state statute unconstitutional or, conversely, a state supreme court has declared a federal statute unconstitutional or has upheld its own state statute against a challenge that it violated the federal constitution. In all other situations in California or in the federal courts, appeals to the highest court are discretionary, by writ of certiorari. The court decides for itself what are the most important questions that deserve its attention and will refuse to hear appeals from cases raising issues deemed not as crucial. In this way it supervises the administration of law by the lower courts on an ad hoc basis. At the other end of the spectrum, in New York appeals to the state's highest court are as of right in a great many cases provided for by statute. The primary function of the highest court in New York appears to be to assure that the case was correctly decided. It is necessary to check carefully the statutes of the system in which you are appearing to determine what specific scope of review is given to those appellate courts.

II. CHOOSING THE PROPER COURT

A. SUBJECT MATTER JURISDICTION

1. IN GENERAL

§ 2-1. Principles Governing

The first question that you must address when deciding where to bring your action is which courts have the requisite power to decide the type of controversy involved in your case. This requirement typically is stated in terms of whether the court has subject matter jurisdiction. With one exception (see § 2-5, infra), questions of subject matter jurisdiction are determined by referring to federal and state statutes, which authorize jurisdiction over particular types of cases.

In the state courts typically the statutes establishing the different courts in the state will set each court's subject matter jurisdiction boundaries. State subject matter jurisdiction constraints exist primarily as a means of regulating the flow of judicial business before the state courts. In some instances jurisdiction will be distributed according to the type of proceeding involved, as in the case of probate proceedings or criminal matters. Amount limitations also may serve to delineate court boundaries. For example, matters involving less than $1,000 may be assigned to Municipal Court, while matters involving more than

[7]

that amount will be heard by the Superior Court.
Few problems arise in applying these limitations.
The question is not whether you can bring your
action in state court, but which of the existing
state courts is authorized to hear your case.

The approach changes when federal subject
matter jurisdiction is involved. Federal courts
are courts of *general* jurisdiction. That is to say,
all federal district courts are treated as trial courts
of equal jurisdictional power; there is no division
among the federal courts as to what cases can be
tried in which tribunal. A federal district court
may entertain an action based on almost any area
of the law. The one exception to this principle
is the existence of specialized federal courts to
handle special matters, such as the Tax Court, the
Court of Claims and the Bankruptcy Court. However, even in those cases the plaintiff typically has
the option of filing suit in the specialized federal
court or in the federal district court. The problem in defining federal court subject matter jurisdiction arises because Article III, Section 2 of
the U. S. Constitution limits federal jurisdiction
solely to those matters specifically listed in that
clause. All other controversies are left to the
state courts to decide. Further, the Congress in
enacting enabling legislation for the judicial power clause is under no obligation to give the federal
courts all the jurisdiction authorized under the
Constitution and in some instances it has refrain-

ed from so doing. Thus, the issue is not in which federal court should you lodge your case, but whether any federal court can entertain the controversy.

There may be a number of reasons why you may prefer a federal forum. The applicable rules governing the procedures to be followed during the trial may be more liberal than the state rules. The federal court may be more conveniently located than the nearest state court. Federal judges often are perceived as having more expertise than their state counterparts. Further, they may be subject to fewer outside pressures since they are not elected but are appointed for life. Whatever the reason, federal subject matter jurisdiction is strictly limited. If you want to use the federal courts as a forum, you must determine whether the federal courts have been given *concurrent* jurisdiction with the states over your particular controversy. This inquiry may present a complex constitutional, as well as a statutory, problem and it often has been the subject of litigation.

Before turning to an examination of federal subject matter jurisdiction, a distinction must be drawn between *original* and *appellate* jurisdiction. Courts having original jurisdiction are courts of first instance—that is where you go to obtain a trial of your case. Courts having appellate jurisdiction function as reviewing courts and the case may be brought to them only on appeal from an order or judgment in a lower court. Thus, any inquiry into subject matter jurisdiction must consider not only whether the court has been given the power to hear a certain controversy, but also whether it is a trial or an appellate tribunal. Further, in a few instances the jurisdiction statute will give a particular court *exclusive* jurisdiction over a particular type of controversy so that only that court will be a proper forum. For example, the federal courts have been given exclusive jurisdiction over suits based on patents and copyrights (28 U.S.C.A. § 1338(a)), and over all proceedings in bankruptcy (28 U.S.C.A. § 1334) and no action on those matters can be brought in the state courts. Conversely, probate and divorce matters are within the exclusive jurisdiction of the state courts and, in most instances only properly brought before certain specialized state courts established to handle those cases. Interestingly, the exclusive jurisdiction of probate and family courts is not of statutory origin. It is an historic division of authority that the other state and federal courts have continued to recognize, although not required to do so as a matter of statutory or constitutional law.

A brief introduction to the main types of general federal jurisdiction and its restraints follows. Readers interested in a more detailed review should refer to D. Currie, *Federal Jurisdiction in a Nutshell,* 90–148 (1976), or C. Wright, *Federal Courts* 63–168 (3d ed. 1976).

2. FEDERAL JURISDICTION

§ 2-2. Federal Question Jurisdiction

The Constitution provides for federal court jurisdiction whenever the case "arises under" federal law. Many federal statutes create the right to sue for the violation of the rights or duties enumerated therein (i. e., federal antitrust or securities laws), and at the same time explicitly grant jurisdiction to the federal courts to hear those matters. In this way *special federal question jurisdiction* is established. The Congress also has provided in 28 U.S.C.A. § 1331, that the federal courts may take jurisdiction over any civil action arising under the Constitution, laws or treaties of the United States, and in which more than $10,000 is involved (see § 2–4, infra). Actions against the United States government or federal officials or agencies need not meet the $10,000 minimum requirement. The chief problem in invoking *general federal question jurisdiction* has been in determining how to apply the "arising under" requirement. Stated most simply, a right or immunity created by federal law must be a basic element of the plaintiff's cause of action, not merely a collateral issue or introduced by way of defense.

[11]

The notion that a case does not "arise under" federal law if the defendant introduces the federal issue was established by the United States Supreme Court in Louisville & Nashville R. R. v. Mottley, 211 U.S. 149 (1908). No language in the constitution mandates that interpretation. Nonetheless, the Court has firmly embraced the "well-pleaded complaint" rule on numerous occasions. A plaintiff can invoke federal court jurisdiction only when the statement of his claim, properly pleaded, shows that it is based on federal law. Emphasis is placed on what are the proper and necessary elements of a cause of action. Jurisdiction is not proper if the plaintiff improperly anticipates a defense or if it is based on the defendant's counterclaim. Although the well-pleaded complaint rule has been criticized, it remains the governing principle in federal question cases. It has been extended to declaratory judgment actions to require an inquiry in those suits as to how the action would have been pleaded but for the availability of declaratory relief in order to determine whether a federal question appears properly on the face of the complaint.

§ 2-3. Diversity of Citizenship Jurisdiction

The federal district courts are given original jurisdiction over cases involving citizens of different states under Article III, Section 2 of the Constitution. In addition, the enabling legislation, 28 U.S.C.A. § 1332, provides for diversity jurisdiction in suits between citizens of a state and foreign citizens or governments, 28 U.S.C.A. § 1332(a), (2) (3), but limits all diversity jurisdiction to disputes involving more than $10,000 (see § 2–4, infra). No federal jurisdiction is provided for actions between two aliens or when one of the parties is a United States citizen but has no state citizenship. State courts are the only available fora in those cases. A further restriction on the invocation of federal diversity jurisdiction is the interpretation of the statute given by the Supreme Court in Strawbridge v. Curtiss, 7 U.S. (3 Cranch) 267 (1806). The Court ruled that there must be complete diversity; in multi-party suits no plaintiff can share the same state citizenship with any defendant.

State citizenship is determined on the basis of a party's domicile, as opposed to mere residence. A person will be found to be domiciled in a state if she maintains her principal establishment there. Domicile requires the physical presence of a residence within the state plus the intention to make that residence your present home. It is not required that the party whose domicile is in issue intend to reside there permanently. Persons such as servicemen, prisoners, and students can establish a domicile even though they may be only involuntarily or temporarily residing in a state. The key is whether they intend to maintain their principal establishment there for the time being. In the case of corporations, the diversity statute provides for citizenship both where the corporation is incorporated and where it maintains its principal place of business. 28 U.S.C.A. § 1332(c). This provision acts to narrow diversity jurisdiction as a corporation is deemed a citizen of two states.

Whether diversity of citizenship exists is determined as of the time the action is commenced. The citizenship of the parties at the time the cause of action arose or during the later course of the proceedings is not determinative. Thus, the plaintiff can change domicile just before filing suit in order to create diversity. In a few cases such tactics have been challenged on the ground that they violate the federal anticollusive jurisdiction statute, 28 U.S.C.A. § 1359. However, most courts have refused to consider the motives behind the plaintiff's actions and have inquired only into the question whether a legal domicile has been established.

Diversity of citizenship jurisdiction is under serious attack. The historic premise for diversity was that it allowed entry into the federal courts in order to protect out of state residents from any potential prejudice that might exist in the local fora. There is serious question whether any modern justification for diversity exists and most commentators and courts agree that the historic rationale no longer presents a valid concern. With

[*14*]

the caseload of the federal courts constantly increasing, it is not surprising that several proposals currently are pending before the Congress to eliminate or seriously curtail diversity jurisdiction.

§ 2–4. Amount in Controversy

As a means of limiting access to the federal courts, the Congress has included amount in controversy requirements in some of the jurisdictional statutes, such as the general federal question and diversity provisions. Since 1958 in cases invoking those jurisdictional bases the matter in controversy must exceed $10,000, exclusive of interest and costs. This prerequisite acts to assure that only the more significant cases (in terms of size) reach the federal courts and in this way it controls the federal courts caseload. Further, it protects small litigants from what may be the increased costs of federal court litigation.

Perhaps because amount in controversy requirements are merely judicial housekeeping measures and not constitutional barriers, the test for ascertaining whether they have been met is quite liberal. If the sum claimed by the plaintiff is made in good faith and it is not clear to a legal certainty that more than $10,000 will not be recovered, the requirement is met. In actions seeking injunctive relief, the amount in controversy may be established by looking at the cost to the plaintiff if relief is denied or the amount it will

[*15*]

cost the defendant to comply with the proposed
injunction. The burden is placed on the defendant to show that the minimum amount is not involved. If it becomes apparent during the course
of the trial or at the entry of the judgment that
less than the requisite amount is involved, the
case need not be dismissed for lack of subject matter jurisdiction at that time. Rather, the statutes
provide that the court may assess costs against
the plaintiff. 28 U.S.C.A. §§ 1331(b), 1332(b).
In practice this measure is used infrequently and
typically will be applied only when the plaintiff
has acted in clear bad faith.

The largest difficulties in applying the amount
in controversy requirements have arisen in cases
involving multiple parties and multiple claims.
The problem is how to value the amount in controversy when some of the claims are jurisdictionally
sufficient and others are not, or when no individual claim involves the requisite amount, but the
sum total of all the claims being asserted is more
than $10,000. Most commonly, the issue is
phrased in terms of whether aggregation is proper,
although the question whether a claim seeking
less than the minimum allowed can be heard when
the court already has before it a jurisdictionally
sufficient claim may be analyzed in terms of
whether the court should exercise ancillary or
pendent jurisdiction. See § 2–5, infra.

The general rules governing aggregation of claims are the following. In a simple two-party action between A and B, A may join all the claims related and unrelated she has against B and aggregation will be allowed. When aggregation of only A's claims is involved there is at least the possibility that if they are all valid, more than the jurisdictional minimum will be recovered. However, A will not be allowed to aggregate her claims with any counterclaims made by B in order to meet the applicable amount in the controversy requirement. To allow aggregation in that situation would permit the parties to consent to subject matter jurisdiction indirectly and that is impermissible. Further, if both claims are valid, the claim and counterclaim will set-off one another and there will be no possibility that more than $10,000 will be recovered. Finally, to allow jurisdiction based on any allegation made by the defendant violates the well-pleaded complaint rule, which requires that jurisdiction be tested on the basis of plaintiff's allegations alone.

In multiple party litigation in which two plaintiffs (A & B) sue C or one plaintiff, A, sues two defendants (C & D) and in which no one claim meets the amount restrictions, the courts have upheld jurisdiction only when both plaintiffs, A & B or both defendants, C & D, have a "joint and common interest" in the subject matter of the action, rather than a "several interest." This test also has been applied to class actions: each class member must possess a claim above $10,000, unless the members possess a joint and common interest in the action. Snyder v. Harris, 394 U.S. 332 (1970).

What constitutes a joint and common interest has plagued the courts and commentators for years and is incapable of precise delineation. Suffice it to say that the requirement will be satisfied only in a small class of cases in which the law essentially has ruled that various interests are to be treated as one. For example, a husband and wife are deemed to hold a joint interest in their home in community property states. Partners similarly possess a joint interest in the partnership assets. However, the fact that the parties are united in interest in terms of desiring the same relief or resisting the same claims does not give them a joint and common interest. A parent seeking damages for injuries to his minor child and reimbursement for the medical expenses that were incurred cannot aggregate those claims so as to be able to obtain federal court jurisdiction. The personal injury claim belongs to the child and the medical expenses claim represents damage to the parent; the parent-child relationship in itself does not create a joint and common interest in the action. Consequently, it is necessary to analyze the facts of each case carefully in light of past precedent to determine whether this requirement has been met.

[*18*]

§ 2-5. Ancillary and Pendent Jurisdiction

Ancillary and pendent jurisdiction are the only examples of nonstatutory subject matter jurisdiction in the federal courts. The concepts were developed by the courts for use in multiple claim actions in order to permit entire disputes to be tried in the federal courts, thereby avoiding multiple actions. Both types of jurisdiction require the presence in the suit of at least one claim that is sufficient under one of the statutory bases for subject matter jurisdiction. Jurisdiction then may be allowed over some otherwise jurisdictionally insufficient claim if that claim arises out of the same core of aggregate fact or, stated alternatively, if both claims arise out of a common nucleus of operative fact. Given the liberal claim and party joinder provisions in the federal rules, these bases for jurisdiction frequently are invoked.

The assertion of this jurisdictional power is deemed constitutional under Article III, section 2 because the courts merely are defining what will be deemed "a case or controversy" in a multiple claim situation. The rationale supporting the extension of federal court jurisdiction to ancillary or pendent claims is primarily one of judicial economy—to rule otherwise would require the plaintiff to file two suits, one in federal and the other in state court. Further, the availability of pendent jurisdiction makes the federal court a viable alternative to the state courts in which all the claims could be joined.

The question whether ancillary or pendent jurisdiction exists in a given case requires a two-part analysis. This two-step analysis was first suggested by the Supreme Court in United Mine Workers of America v. Gibbs, 383 U.S. 715 (1966). The first question that must be asked is whether the claim meets the standard for asserting this type of jurisdiction—is there a common nucleus of operative fact between the jurisdictionally sufficient and insufficient claims? Illustratively, an action asserting a federal antitrust claim and a state unfair competition claim usually will meet this standard. Many of the facts that must be proven to show unfair competition also will aid in demonstrating price-fixing or a monopoly, which would violate the federal law. On the other hand, a slander claim will require proof of different facts than a personal injury claim. This is true even if the defendant allegedly slandered the plaintiff immediately after he ran into her with his automobile so that the events giving rise to the claims were part of a series. Once the court determines that it has the power to decide the entire case, it then must decide whether taking the otherwise jurisdictionally insufficient claim will foster judicial economy and will be fair to the parties. Thus, the actual assertion of ancillary or pendent jurisdiction is discretionary.

A wide range of factors may be taken into account in deciding this discretionary issue and the court may review the exercise of its discretion throughout the case. For example, if the claims that independently meet subject matter jurisdiction requirements are dismissed at an early stage in the proceedings, judicial economy may suggest that the ancillary or pendent claims also should be dismissed and the parties left to the state courts on those issues. If the state issues presented by a proposed ancillary or pendent claim are peculiarly difficult or novel, jurisdiction may be declined in order to allow the state courts to rule on the questions. If the presence of the additional claims or parties would produce jury confusion that may not be controlled in other ways, jurisdiction may be refused. In any case in which pendent or ancillary jurisdiction is not allowed, only those additional claims will be dismissed, the federal court will continue to hear the jurisdictionally proper claims before it.

Courts frequently confuse the terms ancillary and pendent and you should not be misled by the denomination they utilize. Although the test governing the assertion of both ancillary and pendent jurisdiction is the same, the terms technically apply to different types of situations. Historically, pendent jurisdiction was invoked when the question presented was whether a state law claim could be asserted by a party who already was presenting a federal question claim. Ancillary jurisdiction pertained when diversity jurisdiction was the basis of the sufficient claim and the proposed ancillary claim was being asserted by someone other than the person who alleged the jurisdictionally sufficient claim. Thus, if the plaintiff asserts two claims, one of which is based on a federal question and the other on state law, then pendent jurisdiction should be invoked. When the second claim is asserted by a different party than the original claimant, as when a counterclaim, third-party claim or intervention claim is presented, ancillary jurisdiction pertains.

In recent years the lower federal courts have stretched pendent and ancillary jurisdiction concepts to embrace many new multi-party situations. Pendent jurisdiction has been expanded to include situations involving party, as well as claim joinder, developing what is referred to as pendent-party jurisdiction. A plaintiff may sue two defendants, asserting a jurisdictionally sufficient claim against one and a related but insufficient claim against the other (a claim for less than $10,000 in a diversity case, or a state claim in a federal question action). If the court finds that the claims arise out of a common nucleus of operative fact, pendent-party jurisdiction may be allowed over that otherwise jurisdictionally insufficient claim against that party. A similar result may occur when two or more plaintiffs join in a suit against a defendant. The validity of pendent-party jurisdiction is somewhat in doubt because of a recent Supreme Court decision, Aldinger v. Howard, 427 U.S. 1 (1976). Although the case rested on statutory grounds, language in the opinion may be taken as a signal that the Supreme Court does not favor this extension of jurisdiction. Additionally, the attempt to use ancillary jurisdiction concepts to authorize a plaintiff to assert an otherwise jurisdictionally insufficient claim against a third-party defendant, was struck down as violative of the diversity statute's requirement of complete diversity. Owen Equipment & Erection Co. v. Kroger, 98 S.Ct. 2396 (1978). Thus, the continued expansion of ancillary and pendent jurisdiction seems halted, at least temporarily.

§ 2–6. Removal Jurisdiction

When concurrent jurisdiction is placed in the federal and state courts, the plaintiff may choose in which one to file suit. If plaintiff opts for state court, the defendant may be able to get the suit to the federal court in that district if the defendant can show that the case falls within the special federal statute designed for that purpose, 28 U.S. C.A. § 1441. In a two-party single claim action there are four prerequisites to removal. First, removal jurisdiction is derivative so that removal will be allowed only when the action properly was before the state court in the first instance. Second, removal is proper only if the federal court would have had jurisdiction had the plaintiff opt-

ed to begin the action there. 28 U.S.C.A. § 1441
(a). In light of the well-pleaded complaint rule,
see § 2–2, supra, this means that removal cannot
be based on a federal question in the defendant's
answer or on the fact that a federal counterclaim
is being asserted. The plaintiff's complaint must
present a basis for federal court jurisdiction.
However, the fact that venue would have been
improper in the federal court will not preclude
removal. Only jurisdictional defects will act as
a bar. Third, only defendants can remove. 28
U.S.C.A. § 1441(a). Fourth, in cases based on
diversity of citizenship only non-resident defendants can remove. 28 U.S.C.A. § 1441(b).

A major problem in deciding whether removal
is proper occurs in multi-claim or multi-party disputes in which some but not all the claims being
asserted meet the above requirements. In order
to prevent the plaintiff from blocking the defendant's option simply by including some non-removable claims or parties and to make the defendant's
choice of the federal court a viable one, the removal statute specifically provides for the removal of the entire action under these circumstances.
28 U.S.C.A. § 1441(c). Removal is permissible if
the defendant can show the existence of a claim
that meets the four general requirements for removal and that that claim is "separate and independent" from the other non-removable claims.
However, once the action is removed, the federal

court must consider whether it should exercise its discretion to remand to the state court the otherwise jurisdictionally insufficient claims. That decision involves an analysis of the relatedness of the claims and of whether it will be judicially economical to try all the claims in one action—an analysis akin to that utilized when deciding whether pendent or ancillary jurisdiction may be proper. See § 2–5, supra. Removal in multiclaim actions thus appears to require almost schizoid determinations by the court—on the one hand the movant's claim must be separate, on the other it must be related—and, not surprisingly, it has resulted in some confusing court decisions. Stated most simply, the separate and independent prerequisite focuses on whether more than one claim is presented on which multiple recoveries are possible or whether the complaint presents alternative and mutually exclusive theories of recovery. See, e. g., Twentieth Century-Fox Film Corp. v. Taylor, 239 F.Supp. 913 (S.D.N.Y.1965). If the latter is the case, the requirement will not be met. The court's discretionary inquiry on the remand question focuses on how much factual or evidentiary overlap exists between the claims.

Removal jurisdiction may raise serious federalism concerns as it presents a situation in which the federal court is taking a case away from a state court, albeit at the request of a party. This fact is emphasized by the removal procedure, itself. The defendant in the state court action files the removal petition in the federal court. See 28 U.S.C.A. § 1446(a). A copy of the petition is filed simultaneously in the state court and that act effectuates the removal. As stated in the federal removal statute, "the State court shall proceed no further unless and until the case is remanded." 28 U.S.C.A. § 1446(c). The desire to afford the defendant the opportunity to invoke federal jurisdiction is deemed to outweigh concerns about the potential impact of removal on federal-state court relations. Nonetheless, a federal court deciding whether to remand some state claims that are before it only because of the operation of Section 1441(c) may be influenced by federalism notions to return to the state court those claims not clearly or inextricably entwined with the jurisdictionally sufficient claims.

B.   VENUE

§ 2–7.   General Principles Governing

Venue is a statutory requirement designed to regulate the flow of judicial business within a particular court system and to identify a convenient forum for the parties to litigate their dispute. In the federal court system, venue provisions set out the district or districts in a given state in which suit may be brought, assuming subject matter and personal jurisdiction requirements are

met. In state court systems, venue statutes typically refer to the proper county in which to bring
the action. Once you have determined whether
you can file your action in state or federal court,
§§ 2–1—2–4, supra, and in which states personal
jurisdiction may be obtained over the defendant,
§§ 2–10—2–20, infra, you must consult the applicable venue statutes in order to further identify
which courts within those judicial systems are
permissible fora.

Although the types of venue statutes vary,
some general discussion of their characteristics
may be helpful. A common provision that is
utilized places venue for transitory causes of action at the residence of the defendant. See Cal.
Civ.Proc.Code § 395(a). The residence of a corporation has been established statutorily as the
place of its incorporation, any place in which it is
doing business or, in some states, the corporation's
principal place of business. See 28 U.S.C.A. §
1391(c), Cal.Civ.Proc.Code § 395.5. More specific venue provisions may be tied to the kind of
action being brought (i. e. tort, contract) and may
identify the locale of specific events (i. e. the per-
formance of the contract, tortious injury) as a
convenient place to bring suit. In the federal system, the general venue statute provides for venue
at defendant's residence, where the cause of action arose and, in diversity of citizenship cases,
also at the plaintiff's residence. 28 U.S.C.A. §

1391(a), (b). In cases in which more than one
venue may be proper, the plaintiff can choose
where to file suit.

The propriety of the venue is determined at the
outset of the action. If additional claims are filed,
such as third-party claims or intervention claims,
the venue requirements typically will not be applied to those claims. Courts commonly invoke
notions of waiver or ancillary venue in these circumstances. When a counterclaim is asserted
against the plaintiff, it is said that by filing suit
plaintiff consented to the convenience of the forum. In cases in which additional claims are allowed in the court on a theory of ancillary jurisdiction, the courts frequently note that ancillary
venue applies. All these approaches to venue over
additional claims rest on the sound premise that
if the forum is established as a convenient one at
the outset, it will remain so for the parties and all
their claims. Thus, unlike subject matter and
personal jurisdiction, venue need not be tested
each time a claim is added to the action.

§ 2–8. Local Action Principle

A common distinction that is drawn in venue
statutes is the difference between a local and a
transitory action. Local actions are those which
involve ownership of, possession of, or injury to
real property. Transitory actions encompass all
other suits. Historically, because of the desire to

have juries who were familiar with the facts of the case, local actions could be brought only in the county in which the land was situated. Transitory actions were not so restricted.

The local action principle may be viewed as a venue rule, regulating the business of the courts within a state. When applied across state lines its significance increases, as it becomes entwined with notions of state sovereignty over property within the borders. Based on the local action principle, the United States Supreme Court has held that a court in the county or district in which land is situated may refuse to give full faith and credit to the judgment or decree of another state's court which affects the title to that land, even though the parties were within the personal jurisdiction of the forum court at the time the judgment was entered. Fall v. Eastin, 215 U.S. 1 (1909). This seems to elevate the local action principle to constitutional magnitude, an anomolous result in our federal system. Whether the case remains good law may never be decided because all recent state decisions have ruled that full faith and credit will be given, even though it is not required.

C. PERSONAL JURISDICTION

§ 2–9. Introduction: The Two-pronged Test

The doctrine of personal jurisdiction raises the question whether a court has the power to render a binding, enforceable judgment defining or declaring the rights and duties of the parties. As to plaintiffs, the very act of seeking relief always has been supposed to constitute a submission to jurisdiction, warranting a judgment against them. When the proposed defendant resides in and is present in the state in which the court is sitting, the question has posed few problems; power is assumed to exist as each state has sovereignty over all things and persons within its borders. In those cases the question becomes whether jurisdiction has been exercised properly and upon adequate notification.

Historically, the only real difficulty in applying these territorial principles involved corporations, since corporations are only legal constructs and have no tangible existence and thus no visible situs. The corporation problem was first solved by holding that a corporation always was subject to the jurisdiction of the courts under whose laws it was incorporated. The courts later added to this notion the rule that a corporation also was subject to suit when it had "consented" expressly or impliedly to be sued in a particular state. See § 2–15, infra. This consent theory quickly verged on the fictitious so courts added another concept seeking to equate corporations and natural persons. Because the physical presence of a person was deemed enough, a corporation was declared "present" and thus within a given state's jurisdiction when the extent and continuity of its business activities in the state seemed large enough to equate activity with presence. Under that theory, the discontinuance of corporate activities, just as the departure of an individual, terminated the state's jurisdiction to enter a binding, enforceable judgment.

The major jurisdictional problems and developments have centered on the issue whether a court can assert personal jurisdiction over a defendant not found within the state. To answer this question usually requires two steps. First, you must inquire whether there is a statute (commonly referred to as a long-arm statute) authorizing the assertion of personal jurisdiction outside the state borders under circumstances similar to your case. Second, you must consider whether the application of the statute to the case at hand meets constitutional standards. Both these tests must be met for each defendant in an action, as well as any additional parties who later may be joined.

The development of state long-arm statutes and of the constitutional standard applied to extra-territorial assertions of personal jurisdiction has undergone several twists and turns. Its complete study requires an analysis of Supreme Court decisions, a close look at a number of the statutes that have been adopted, and a review of lower court decisions that have applied and interpreted these developments. Finally, because of a new 1977 Supreme Court decision, Shaffer v. Heitner, 433 U.S. 186 (1977), some evaluation must be made of what to expect in the future. After an abbreviated history of the law before 1977, the primary focus in this Nutshell will be on modern jurisdictional theory under the Supreme Court's new decision. The reader may wish to refer to the more complete treatment of prior history in A. Ehrenzweig and D. Louisell, *Jurisdiction in a Nutshell* (3d ed. 1973).

1. STATUTORY SOURCES OF JURISDICTIONAL POWER

a. State Courts

§ 2–10. Types of Long-arm Statutes

The first thing that you must do when you are seeking to bring an action against a non-resident defendant is to determine if there is a state statute authorizing the assertion of extraterritorial jurisdiction and if your case meets the prerequisites set out in the statute. Without statutory authorization, personal jurisdiction cannot be asserted.

Although state long-arm statutes are many and varied, a brief description may be helpful. The primary differentiating characteristic between various long-arm statutes is the amount of detailed requirements or categories that are set out. At one end of the spectrum are those permitting the assertion of jurisdiction whenever the defendant has the necessary minimum contacts with the state and jurisdiction would not be contrary to the constitution or laws of the United States. See, e. g., R.I.Gen.L. § 9–5–33, Cal.Civ.Proc.Code § 410.10. These vague statutory standards allow the courts to stretch their jurisdiction to its furthest possible limits. They also are easy to apply in an era of increasing travel and expanded business dealings since the statute can change with the times. However, this fluidity has drawbacks. Every jurisdiction problem becomes a constitutional one and the prognosis for when jurisdiction will be upheld is more difficult to make because of the vagueness of the standard.

At the other end of the spectrum, some states have listed in great detail the kinds of activities on the part of the defendant for which extraterritorial jurisdiction may be asserted. For example, all fifty states had non-resident motorist statutes, providing for the assertion of jurisdiction over non-residents who have driven into the state and caused an accident there. Other common acts for which long-arm jurisdiction may be asserted are:

[*33*]

the transaction of business in the state, contracting to supply goods or services in the state, the commission of a tortious act in the state, the commission of a tortious act outside the state that causes injury in the state, coupled with some other business activity of defendant in the state, and the ownership, use or the possession of real property in a state. See, e. g., N.Y.C.P.L.R. 302(a); Uniform Interstate & Int'l Pro.Act § 1.03. Other states have focused on the kind of action being brought (i. e. contract, tort) and have set out the conduct on the part of the defendant that will justify the assertion of long-arm jurisdiction in those types of suits. See, e. g., N.C.Gen.Stat. § 1–75–4. If an action does not fit into any of the categories listed in these more specific statutes, jurisdiction must be denied.

b.   FEDERAL COURTS

§ 2–11.   General Rules Governing

Although the Congress could enact legislation governing the assertion of personal jurisdiction by the federal courts, with few exceptions, see § 2–12, infra, it has not done so. Federal Rule 4 (e) specifically provides that in the absence of federal legislation, each federal court must refer to the statutes and rules governing out of state service that exist in the state in which it is sitting. Federal courts may utilize state long-arm statutes or any state statute allowing the attachment of property owned by non-residents in order to obtain jurisdiction over a non-resident defendant. If those statutes do not exist or do not apply to the facts of the case at hand, then, in the absence of some special federal statute, personal jurisdiction cannot be obtained. Thus, the ability of a federal court to enter a binding, enforceable judgment against a non-resident defendant typically is the same as the state courts of the state in which it is sitting.

§ 2–12. Specialized Provisions

With one exception, the few federal long-arm provisions that exist are part of statutes establishing particular federal causes of action. For example, in actions brought under the antitrust or the federal securities laws there are no geographic boundaries to the federal courts jurisdiction. 15 U.S.C.A. §§ 4 and 78aa. Similarly, in federal interpleader actions in which a stakeholder with a limited fund to which there are conflicting claims is seeking a ruling as to how the fund should be distributed, a federal statute authorizes nationwide service of process, eliminating any limitations on the federal courts personal jurisdiction. 28 U.S.C.A. § 2361. Although these provisions are few in number, it is wise in actions based on federal law to check the statute on which you are suing to determine if a special long-arm provision is available.

The one other, more general, federal long-arm provision worth noting is Federal Rule 4(f) authorizing service of process within one hundred miles of the federal courthouse for certain additional parties to the action. In many instances this 100-mile bulge provision will not act extraterritorially as the court may be so situated that a one hundred mile radius is still within the state. However, in other cases the application of the provision will result in long-arm jurisdiction being obtained, despite the absence of any applicable state long-arm statute.

2.   THE STANDARD FOR ASSERTING PERSONAL JURISDICTION

a.   JURISDICTIONAL THEORY PRIOR TO 1977

§ 2–13.   Sovereignty as a Basis

Personal jurisdiction doctrine originally rested on notions of sovereignty. Since each state had exclusive power over all persons within its borders, it could render binding judgments in any suits brought against those persons. This jurisdiction typically was referred to as *in personam*. In personam jurisdiction was premised on the presence of the individual defendant in the state at the time the action was commenced. It mattered not whether the defendant's presence was temporary, as in the case of a transient, or more permanent. On the other hand, no in personam jurisdiction was allowed over persons outside the state borders, as that would violate another state's sovereignty. A valid in personam judgment was entitled to full faith and credit in all the sister states under Art. IV, § 1 of the United States Constitution.

The state also had sovereign power over all the property within its borders and it was held that a state court could render a valid and enforceable judgment concerning the ownership of or title to in-state property, regardless of the whereabouts of the defendant. This form of personal jurisdiction was termed *in rem*. Because of the state's exclusive control over the property, any judgment entered in such an action would "bind the world" and other states would be required to give it full faith and credit.

Notions of sovereignty were not as limited as the preceding description might suggest. For example, in personam jurisdiction based on the defendant's domicile and, even his national citizenship was upheld. It was reasoned that the sovereign could command certain obligations and duties from its citizens even when they were not physically present in the jurisdiction. Similarly, in cases involving the marital status of a resident plaintiff and a defendant who no longer was a resident, jurisdiction was upheld based on the notion that the state had sovereign power over the legal status of its domiciliaries and necessarily

[37]

must be able to render a binding decree on the status of its resident plaintiff. Finally, non-residents who owned property within a state were deemed within the state's in personam jurisdiction on causes of action arising out of that property. A non-resident landlord could be sued for injuries caused by the failure to maintain the property in a safe condition. The state's sovereign control over the property allowed it to enter an enforceable judgment against the landlord if he wanted the privilege of owning property in the state.

The most important expansion in the law of sovereignty as it applied to personal jurisdiction came with the development of *quasi in rem* jurisdiction. In quasi in rem jurisdiction property within a state is used as a vehicle to reach the defendant in order to adjudicate personal rights unrelated to that property. The state asserts its sovereign power by attaching or seizing the property at the commencement of the action. Then, utilizing the fiction that the property is a manifestation of the defendant, the court adjudicates the personal claim before it. If the defendant enters to defend, he submits himself to the in personam jurisdiction of the court and a binding judgment for the full amount claimed can be entered in the event that the plaintiff wins. If the defendant does not appear and defaults, the judgment will be limited to the value of the property attached, as, in keeping with the fiction, that is the limit of the state's sovereign power. No full faith and credit will be given to the judgment beyond that amount. The plaintiff must begin an entirely new action in order to obtain further relief.

Attachment of the property at the commencement was crucial to this form of jurisdiction. It substantiated the state's claim of power and, by preventing the property from being moved or sold during the action, it ensured the enforcement of any judgment the plaintiff might obtain. Pennoyer v. Neff, 95 U.S. 714 (1877). Finally, it was felt that attachment served as a means of notifying the defendant of the proceedings.

Although the doctrine of quasi in rem jurisdiction originated in cases involving real property, where the state's sovereignty was deeply rooted in history, it gradually was expanded to apply to movable property, intangibles, and even contingent obligations. These latter developments have caused a great degree of controversy and their validity is in serious question today. See § 2–14, infra.

§ 2–14. Intangibles and Contingent Obligations

The assertion of quasi in rem jurisdiction based on the presence of intangibles and contingent obligations in the state raised the problem of how to identify their situs. For example, bank deposits were deemed to be located at the bank with which the defendant did business and stock frequently was deemed to be present wherever the stock certificates were located. One of the most controversial applications of quasi in rem jurisdiction in this context is the rule developed by the United States Supreme Court that a debt resides with the debtor. Harris v. Balk, 198 U.S. 215 (1904). By locating the debt with the debtor, a creditor (A) may obtain quasi in rem jurisdiction over a non-resident debtor (B) if B is owed money by another person (C) and C comes into A's state and is served with process there. If C contests the fact that a debt is owed to B, then A may not obtain quasi in rem jurisdiction over B. In personam jurisdiction over B would be needed in order to be able to enter a judgment declaring that the debt between B and C exists. New York Life Ins. Co. v. Dunlevy, 241 U.S. 518 (1916). Until that question is decided, there is no property within the state on which the court can base quasi in rem jurisdiction. If C concedes the obligation, then the in-state service of process on C permits the court to apply the fiction that the debt as property of B is within its sovereign reach and thus, it may render a judgment on the unrelated claim of A against B that will be enforceable against that property. Under this reasoning, then, B may be subject to quasi in rem jurisdiction wherever his peripetetic debtor may wander. The non-resident debtor was afforded some protection in this scheme by the fact that the seized debtor had to notify him of the proceedings in order to escape being forced to pay again. However, notice did not affect the original court's jurisdiction, it merely protected C from double liability.

An even more controversial application of quasi in rem jurisdiction was developed in New York where the court applied the analysis just described to allow jurisdiction based on an insurer's contingent obligation to defend and indemnify its insured. Seider v. Roth, 216 N.E.2d 312 (N.Y. 1966). The approach taken was as follows. A, a New York resident, is injured in an automobile accident in some other state by B, a non-resident. B is insured by I, a large corporation doing business in New York, as well as other states. A sues B in New York by attaching I's duty to defend and indemnify. Quasi in rem jurisdiction is allowed because of the state's sovereign power over I. The controversy over this form of attachment lies in the contingent nature of the debt: if the insured is found to be free from negligence, then there is no debt; the debt exists only if the plaintiff wins. Thus, jurisdiction is extended to something that does not yet, and may never, exist. Again, some protection is afforded to the defendant to ameliorate the apparent harshness of this doctrine by allowing him to make a limited appearance and defend on the merits without consenting to in personam jurisdiction. The judgment will be limited to the face amount of the policy.

The two developments just described represent the furthest extensions by the courts of sovereignty as a basis for personal jurisdiction. Even before the Supreme Court's 1977 decision they were called into question. A majority of states refused to follow the lead of New York in the insurance field, and other courts and commentators suggested that the fairness of asserting jurisdiction under these circumstances was of prime importance. In an era that emphasizes fairness as the lynchpin for the assertion of jurisdiction (see § 2–16, infra), theories resting solely on sheer power and fictions regarding the situs of intangibles appear shaky at best.

§ 2–15.   Consent as a Basis

A party always may concede a court's authority to render a binding, enforceable judgment against him. In some cases consent may be explicit, as when it is in a contract, in others notions of waiver will act as implied consent. This may occur by the failure of the defendant to comply with the applicable rules governing the methods of raising jurisdictional objections, see § 2–28, infra. In the case of a non-resident plaintiff faced with counterclaims, the entry into the state to institute the action will be deemed submission to the jurisdiction.

Implied consent prior to the filing of a lawsuit served as a prime basis for asserting in personam jurisdiction over a mobile, business citizenry when a strict application of sovereignty principles would not permit jurisdiction. In the corporate field it was held that a state could exclude a non-resident corporation from doing business in the state. Thus, some states enacted legislation requiring out-of-state businesses to consent to jurisdiction as a condition of doing business by appointing an agent in the state to receive process for them. Other states designated a state official as the agent for receipt of process for non-resident corporations and ruled that all corporations doing business thereafter impliedly consented to suit in the state in actions arising out of their activities there. The fact that the corporation no longer was doing business in the state at the time an action was commenced was immaterial because of its prior implied consent to suit.

In cases involving individuals, implied consent became an important justification for the assertion of jurisdiction over non-resident motorists who were alleged to have harmed resident plaintiffs. Utilizing their state police power (a direct manifestation of state sovereignty), states enacted non-resident motorist or single-act statutes, authorizing their courts to assert in personam jurisdiction over non-resident defendants when their sole contact with the state was the accident giving rise to the action and a resident plaintiff was injured. The fiction utilized was that the defendant had impliedly consented to jurisdiction by driving on the highways once the statute had been promulgated.   Hess v. Pawloski, 274 U.S. 352 (1927).   Despite the movement away from utilizing fictions as the basis for asserting jurisdictions, these statutes should remain valid today as the limited type of jurisdiction they authorize should be permissible even under more modern jurisdictional theories.

§ 2–16.   Minimum Contacts, "Fair Play and Substantial Justice" as a Basis

With the increasing movement of individuals between states and the expansion of corporate activities on a national scale, the limitations of the sovereignty and consent theories became apparent.   Although the courts continued to rely on expanding sovereignty notions as the means of supporting in rem and quasi in rem jurisdiction, increased emphasis was placed on due process as the major limitation on a court's power to assert in personam jurisdiction over a non-resident.

The Supreme Court clearly enunciated the principles underlying a due process approach to in personam jurisdiction in International Shoe Co. v. Washington, 326 U.S. 310 (1945).   The test enunciated by the Court was that the defendant should have sufficient "minimum contacts" with the state so that traditional notions of "fair play and substantial justice" would not be offended by the assertion of jurisdiction. Thus, the Court adopted a fluid, policy oriented test, which requires a detailed analysis of the facts in order to decide what is just in each case.

International Shoe presents a two-pronged test. First, minimum contacts must be shown and second, the court must find that the forum is a fair one in which the defendant will have a full opportunity to be heard. While these two determinations necessarily overlap, they have independent significance and meeting one will not justify ignoring the other. For example, the fact that the forum is convenient in that many of the witnesses and parties are there, does not in itself merit the assertion of jurisdiction. The court still must find that the defendant has the requisite minimum contacts with the state to support jurisdiction. Further, this typically will mean that the defendant has in some way purposefully availed himself of the forum. The minimum contacts test applies to both individual and corporate defendants. However, the courts focus a little more carefully on the fairness aspects of the test, as well as the requirement of purposeful entry, when an individual is involved.

§ 2–17. Balancing Factors: Some Examples

The question of the kind and sufficiency of contacts needed to bring a defendant within the threshold of International Shoe is one that can be answered only imprecisely, since the ultimate decision rests within the discretion of the trial court. Nonetheless, some examples will highlight the kinds of considerations that may tip the balance.

If a corporation or an individual is continuously and systematically entering the state and the cause of action arises out of those in-state activities, then jurisdiction is proper. International Shoe Co. v. Washington, 326 U.S. 310 (1945). Not only are the contacts substantial, but also the forum usually will be convenient for all concerned as the witnesses, evidence, and governing law will be there. This also may be true when the cause of action arises outside the state, but out of activities within the state. Cornelison v. Chaney, 545 P.2d 264 (Cal.1976). At the opposite end of the scale, if the defendant's contacts are only sporadic and the cause of action does not arise out of them, whether it arises within or without the state, minimum contacts will not be found and jurisdiction will not be allowed regardless of the convenience of the forum. Hanson v. Denckla, 357 U.S. 235 (1958). In cases that fall between these two extremes, the decision whether there are sufficient minimum contacts will depend largely on balancing the fairness of the forum against the quality and quantity of the contacts the defendant has had with the state.

In some cases a single act may be sufficient, as in the case of non-resident motorists who cause an injury in the forum state, or in a contract dispute in which the contract involved is the only one into which the defendant has entered. In the former case, the interest of the state in providing a forum for its resident plaintiff and regulating his highways coupled with the fact that the defendant purposefully entered the state, and the convenience of the forum insofar as the evidence is concerned, permits the assertion of jurisdiction consistent with notions of fair play. Hess v. Pawloski, 274 U.S. 352 (1927). In the latter, the type of contract involved (insurance), the amount of activities the defendant undertook in the state in connection with the contract, and a finding that the defendant purposefully entered the state in order to make the contract may justify the assertion of jurisdiction. McGee v. International Life Ins. Co., 355 U.S. 220 (1957). However, in contract disputes the decision as to whether the International Shoe standard has been met often is much more difficult in single act cases. The presumptions in which we indulge in tort cases regarding the burdensomeness on the defendant, the interest of the state in the issue in dispute, and the convenience of the forum may be inappropriate when a contract action is involved. The court may take into account the fact that a resident seller induced the buyer into the contract and into the jurisdiction, or that the plaintiff is a major corporation that has easy access to another more convenient forum and the defendant is an individual for whom it will be very burdensome to defend in the forum state.

In another business context involving single acts, state courts have upheld jurisdiction in products liability actions in which the only proven entry of the defendant into the state was the allegedly defective product that is the subject of the litigation and the product has caused an injury in the state. The fact that the defendant places its products into interstate commerce has permitted the presumption that a continuous stream of products was sent into the state and, in the absence of evidence rebutting that presumption, minimum contacts were found. Since the cause of action arose in the state, the forum was deemed convenient. Gray v. American Radiator & Standard Sanitary Corp., 176 N.E.2d 761 (Ill. 1961). This situation is representative of those cases in which jurisdiction has been stretched to its furthest possible limits for there typically is no positive evidence that the defendant purposefully availed itself of the forum. For all practical purposes the presumption of affirmative entry established by the presence of the defective product in the state will be conclusive. It forces the defendant to prove a negative—that at no other time did it or its products ever enter the state.

The issue whether engaging in interstate commerce, without more, is equal to a purposeful entry into all states in the nation has never been addressed by the Supreme Court. Not surprisingly, some lower courts appear willing to assert jurisdiction to the limits until told to do otherwise; others have not extended their jurisdictional reach this far.

In cases in which the cause of action is unrelated to defendant's continuous activities within the state but it occurs within the state, jurisdiction may be proper depending on other factors indicating the fairness of the forum. For example, jurisdiction was allowed in a products liability suit when the defendant manufacturer sent many of its products into the state even though the product being examined in the case at bar was not part of those that the defendant sent into the jurisdiction. Buckeye Boiler Co. v. Superior Court of Los Angeles County, 458 P.2d 57 (Cal. 1969). The key in deciding the question was the minimal potential burden on the defendant in having to defend in the forum, the convenience of the forum in terms of the witnesses and evidence, and the difficulty for the plaintiff if forced to seek an alternative forum.

On the other hand, if the cause of action not only fails to arise out of the defendant's activities in the forum state, but also arises outside the state, then jurisdiction may be denied because the forum is not sufficiently fair, despite the defendant's other unrelated continuous activities in the state. The fact that defendant sends some of its products into California will not be enough to sustain in personam jurisdiction over a claim for an injury caused in Iowa by a product sent to Iowa. Fisher Governor Co. v. Superior Court, 347 P.2d 1 (Cal.1959). However, it has been held that jurisdiction is proper in such a situation when the product was one purchased from the stream of commerce in the forum state. Singer v. Walker, 209 N.E.2d 68 (N.Y.), cert. denied 382 U.S. 905 (1965). These cases, again, depend on a close consideration of all the factors bearing on the interest of the state in providing a forum, and the relative burdens placed on all the parties should jurisdiction be allowed or denied.

b. JURISDICTIONAL THEORY SINCE 1977

§ 2–18. Shaffer v. Heitner: The Fair Play Standard

In 1977 the Supreme Court decided Shaffer v. Heitner, 433 U.S. 186 (1977), and adopted minimum contacts, fair play and substantial justice as the constitutional standard governing all types of personal jurisdiction. No longer is it sufficient to invoke jurisdiction successfully merely by attaching property in the state or by serving process within the state on a transient individual having no other contacts there. State sovereignty is not a proper basis on which to rest jurisdiction, instead the focus is on whether the defendant's due process rights are infringed by the court's assertion of jurisdiction. A close look at how the Court applied due process to the facts of Shaffer may help to predict how the standard will operate in the future.

The case was a shareholder derivative action brought in Delaware against a corporation and several of its present and former officers and directors. The corporation was incorporated in Delaware, but its principal place of business was Arizona. None of the individual defendants resided in Delaware. Plaintiff alleged that the corporation, while under the guidance of the individual defendants, had engaged in some activities in Oregon that had resulted in damages and fines against it for violating the antitrust laws. Those damages and fines were to the ultimate detriment of the corporation and thus the plaintiff, as a shareholder, sought relief on its behalf for the damage caused by the individual defendants' authorization of the illegal activities. In order to obtain jurisdiction over the non-resident individuals, the plaintiff utilized the state sequestration statute and, invoking a Delaware law declaring the situs of all stock in Delaware corporations to be in that state, seized approximately 82,000 shares of the stock belonging to the defendants by placing stop transfer orders on the books of the corporation. The lower Delaware courts upheld this assertion of quasi in rem jurisdiction, but the Supreme Court reversed.

Applying the International Shoe standard, the Court ruled that the presence of property in the state was not sufficient in and of itself. The cause of action was not related to that property in that the defendants' ownership of stock was not directly tied to their fiduciary relationship to the corporation. Additional contacts were necessary. The Court noted that Delaware had not manifested any particular state interest in that its sequestration statute was a general one, not designed specially for the regulation of its corporations and their officers. Finally, it argued that even if Delaware had manifested a strong state interest and minimum contacts were established, Delaware was not a fair forum in which to hear the dispute. The individual defendants had never purposefully availed themselves of the opportunity to conduct activities in the state or had anything to do with the state. Finally, they had no reason to expect to be brought before a Delaware court as the ownership of stock cannot be deemed to imply consent to suit in the state of incorporation.

§ 2–19. Application of the Current Standard

It will require several years of lower court decisions before the full meaning and impact of Shaffer v. Heitner becomes clear. Nonetheless, some prognoses can be made.

To begin with, although Shaffer involved quasi in rem jurisdiction, the Supreme Court's minimum contacts analysis highlights some factors that also are important in in personam cases. In particular, the Court made clear the necessity of finding a legitimate and clearly manifested state interest in asserting jurisdiction. Additionally, it reemphasized, as an element of fairness, that the defendant must have purposefully entered the forum state at some time, even on unrelated activity, or in some way have directly invoked the benefit or protection of that state's laws. The Supreme Court reiterated the importance of these two points in a 1978 decision, Kulko v. Superior Court of California, 436 U.S. 84 (1978). This renewed emphasis suggests that insofar as courts were interpreting the International Shoe standard as permitting jurisdiction if the forum chosen was not inconvenient for the defendant and a resident plaintiff was involved, that approach no longer will be tolerated. With the exception of products liability cases in which the state interest in providing a forum for resident injured plaintiffs is so well recognized, the defendant may have to have had more than indirect dealings within the state before it will be found fair to bind him to a judgment entered there.

The utilization of the minimum contacts standard in pure in rem cases is not likely to have much effect on the decision to take jurisdiction. In typical in rem actions in which the subject matter of the action is the attached property itself, minimum contacts probably still will be found. Most of these cases involve real property, where the state's traditional interest is well recognized, and because of the tangible, immovable nature of the property, it will be clearly foreseeable to the defendant that jurisdiction might be asserted. The ownership of the property itself will demonstrate that the defendant benefitted from the protection of the laws of the state. Indeed, if land is attached in order to assert quasi in rem jurisdiction, the International Shoe standard also may be met as the type of contact the defendant has with the state may be viewed as so substantial that it would not be unfair to require him to defend there, even on an unrelated cause of action.

The main impact of the Shaffer standard will be in those cases in which movable or intangible property is involved. This is true in both in rem and quasi in rem proceedings, as the nature of the property suggests that the defendant may not knowingly have entered the state or invoked the protection of its laws and that his contact with the state is minimal. In these cases the jurisdictional decision must rest on a careful inquiry into the type of contacts the defendant has had with the state, the interest of the forum in the underlying controversy, whether the plaintiff has another forum available that might be more fair, and the actual burden on the defendant in having to litigate in the forum.

Utilizing this formula, it is quite clear that the attachment of a wandering debtor in order to reach another non-resident debtor, without more, no longer will be permissible. On the other hand, an argument can be made supporting quasi in rem jurisdiction in suits brought against a non-resident allleged tortfeasor through the attachment of his insurance policy. In that situation the fact that the insurance company is clearly doing business in the state and actually will be conducting the defense of the action, the interest of the state in providing a forum for its injured resident, and the protection afforded the named defendant by allowing him to make a limited appearance and restrict his potential liability to the insurance may support a finding that there are sufficient minimum contacts to meet due process concerns. Indeed, since Shaffer the Second Circuit has upheld quasi in rem jurisdiction based on the attachment of insurance, stating that the International Shoe standard is not violated. O'Connor v. Lee-Hy Paving Co., 579 F.2d 194 (2d Cir. 1978). Whether the Supreme Court would agree is open to question. If the actual role of the insurance company is ignored, and the court focuses on the availability of alternative forums—the place where the accident occurred or the defendant's residence—and the lack of any knowing or purposeful contact of the named defendant with the state, jurisdiction appears improper. All of this illustrates the kind of close analysis that now will be necessary in order to decide the preliminary issue of personal jurisdiction.

§ 2–20. Current Utility of the Three Jurisdictional Categories

Although the same constitutional standard must be applied to all types of jurisdiction, the tripartite division of jurisdiction into in rem, quasi in rem, and in personam still serves some useful purposes. On a purely practical level, it is a useful device to identify what is in issue and what contacts may be most relevant. Illustratively, in the pure in rem suit an analysis of whether the facts of the case fit the traditional quiet title pattern typically will demonstrate simultaneously that the constitutional standard has been met.

Quasi in rem jurisdiction also remains a separate and useful jurisdictional category on a much more important level. In those states that do not have long-arm statutes authorizing the assertion of extraterritorial jurisdiction to the furthest constitutional limits, the plaintiff may not be able to fit her case within the specific categories set out in the statute. Even though sufficient minimum contacts could be found to meet due process concerns, the absence of an applicable statute prohibits the assertion of in personam jurisdiction. If an attachment statute exists and the defendant owns some property that is in the state, quasi in rem jurisdiction will be permissible.

Different minimum contact thresholds also may exist depending on the type of jurisdiction that is being asserted. In quasi in rem actions the judgment is limited to the value of the property, and, in many instances, the defendant will be allowed to enter and defend on the merits without submitting to the in personam jurisdiction of the court. These added protections for the defendant may allow a finding that a particular forum meets the International Shoe standard for quasi in rem jurisdiction purposes, even though there are not enough contacts to support the assertion of in personam jurisdiction. Thus, viewing the minimum contacts test as a sliding scale, because of some of the protections afforded a non-resident defendant in a quasi in rem action, it may be that in some of those cases a lower threshold to comply with the minimum contacts requirement will exist than would be true in a pure in personam proceeding.

3.   OTHER JURISDICTIONAL CONSTRAINTS

a.   FURTHER DUE PROCESS LIMITATIONS

§ 2–21.   Notice

Although a case meets both the statutory and constitutional requirements for personal jurisdiction, the suit may be dismissed or the judgment collaterally attacked if insufficient notice is given to the defendant.   The defendant can claim that the proceeding violated due process because without proper notice there was no effective opportunity to be heard.

The importance of notice as an element of due process has made individual service of process the best means of obtaining personal jurisdiction. Thus, although the historic rule in in rem proceedings was that attachment plus publication was a sufficient means of serving process, recent cases have indicated that individual notice must be sent when the identity and location of the defendant is known.   Walker v. City of Hutchison, 352 U.S. 112 (1956).

Individual notice is not a constitutional prerequisite to all actions; the type of notice that must be utilized is decided on a case by case basis. The key in all cases, regardless of the type of jurisdiction involved, is what is practicable, with the emphasis on utilizing the means of notice that is most likely to reach the defendant. The court also may consider the difficulties (cost, as well as impracticability) of locating the defendant and the need for the adjudication in deciding what type of notice to require. Mullane v. Central Hanover Bank & Trust Co., 339 U.S. 306 (1950).

§ 2-22. Freedom from Multiple Liability

An essential element of due process is the notion that the court before whom the parties are appearing has the power to assure the defendant that once a judgment is rendered he will not be subject to double or multiple liability in another court. If the court cannot provide this assurance, and an alternative forum exists where all the interested parties can be joined, then the suit must be dismissed on the defendant's motion even though all other jurisdictional prerequisites are met. For example, a Pennsylvania action to escheat funds held by Western Union as uncollected money orders was dismissed since the Pennsylvania court could not obtain jurisdiction over all the other states that also might claim the funds and thus could not protect the defendant against subsequent liability to those states for the same funds. An alternate forum, the Supreme Court, was available and could provide this assurance. Western Union Tel. Co. v. Commonwealth of Pennsylvania, 368 U.S. 71 (1961).

A serious problem is presented when no ideal forum exists. The Supreme Court has ruled that

the desire to protect the defendant from multiple
liability does not permit the court to bind absent
persons to a judgment, if they are not otherwise
within the court's personal jurisdiction reach. If
personal jurisdiction is not obtained over them,
then the defendant may suffer having to pay
twice. New York Life Ins. Co. v. Dunlevy, 241
U.S. 518 (1916). In order to avoid this occurrence, some courts have applied the minimum contacts standard so as to stretch their personal jurisdiction reach to insure that all the pertinent parties are before the court. See, e. g., Atkinson v.
Superior Court, 316 P.2d 960 (Cal.1957), cert. denied 357 U.S. 569 (1958). Notice requirements
also have been construed in a more flexible manner when to require individual notice would prevent the suit from being maintained and there is
no alternative means of settling as a final matter
defendant's potential liability.

b.   OTHER CONSTITUTIONAL LIMITATIONS

§ 2-23.   Interstate Commerce Clause and First Amendment

A few courts have relied on the interstate commerce clause as a separate limitation on the exercise of extraterritorial jurisdiction by a state. An
attempted assertion of jurisdiction was held to
have a direct and negative impact on interstate
commerce—discouraging it because of a liberal

long-arm statute. Thus, jurisdiction was denied even though the forum appeared to be a fair one under a due process standard. Erlanger Mills, Inc. v. Cohoes Fiber Mills, Inc., 239 F.2d 502 (4th Cir. 1956). A majority of courts have not adopted this standard and it has not had any significant impact on the expansion of personal jurisdiction.

Of more importance is the First Amendment. Some courts have taken account of the Amendment's policy to prevent any possible chilling effect on free speech by suggesting that a higher threshold of minimum contacts must be shown in libel actions against non-resident publishers because of the danger that an infringement of free speech rights otherwise will occur. Other courts have ruled that jurisdiction is proper under traditional due process standards, but first amendment concerns should be handled by the court's power to dismiss for forum non conveniens. Under either approach, the result is that the court's jurisdictional reach may be limited if it is found that to hold otherwise might result in restricting the free circulation of ideas because the forum chosen by the plaintiff is distant and inconvenient for the defendant and the local forum would pose a substantial threat to the publisher.

4.   SERVICE OF PROCESS—THE MEANS OF ASSERTING JURISDICTION

§ 2–24.   Types of Service

Local statutes of the state in which suit is brought determine what type of service may be authorized.   Federal Rule 4 sets out the general rules governing how federal process is served, and it also authorizes the federal courts to make use of any applicable state law methods.   Federal courts may utilize the procedure set out in state long-arm statutes, or in state attachment statutes in actions based on quasi in rem jurisdiction.   Special rules are provided in Fed.Rule 4(i) and in treaties with specific countries as to how service is to be accomplished outside the United States borders.

In general there are three types of service— actual, substituted and constructive.   When actual service is utilized, in hand delivery of the summons and complaint is made.   In the case of a corporate or governmental defendant, the statutes frequently denominate the person who will be authorized to receive actual service.   For corporations this often is the company's general or managing agent, (Fed.Rule 4(d)(3)), for governments it may be a designated official, such as the United States attorney in the district in which suit is brought (Fed.Rule 4(d)(4)–(6)).

Substituted service embraces a wide variety of means of notifying the defendant of the action without personal delivery of the summons and complaint. Most state long-arm statutes, for example, provide for process to be sent to the defendant by registered mail. Similarly, attachment statutes commonly provide for the seizure of the property, with notice being mailed to the owner. The defendant may denominate an in-state person to receive actual process, with mailed notice being sent to him. Process also may be delivered to the defendant's dwelling house and left with a person "of suitable age and discretion." (Fed.Rule 4(d) (1)).

Constructive service,—service by publication— historically was the primary means of service of process on out-of-state defendants in in rem jurisdiction cases. Since the main purpose of service of process is to ensure that the defendant is notified of the action, constructive service now may be permitted only when other more direct means of notice, such as mailing, are not possible. McDonald v. Mabee, 243 U.S. 90 (1917). If the defendant's whereabouts are unknown, and there is no domicile to which service can be delivered, then service by publication may be allowed.

§ 2–25. Impermissible Use of Service

In general the courts have allowed process servers to employ whatever means they feel is necessary to complete personal service on recalcitrant defendants.   However, if the means used not only induced the defendant to accept service, but also enticed him into the jurisdiction and the only basis for the court's personal jurisdiction is service in the state, then the suit may be dismissed.   If a default judgment is entered, it may be collaterally attacked on the ground that jurisdiction was obtained by fraud.   Although this does not raise a constitutional challenge to the original judgment, it generally is upheld as the courts will not validate jurisdiction that is obtained by improper or false means.

§ 2–26.   Immunity from Process

There are certain circumstances when service of process cannot be effectuated on a potential defendant even though he is within the state.   In order to encourage active participation in judicial proceedings so as to have full and fair trials, the courts typically have granted immunity from process to all trial participants who otherwise would be outside the court's jurisdictional reach. The one exception to this rule is in the case of counterclaims against a non-resident original plaintiff.   Immunity is not given in that situation because it is felt that by instituting the action the plaintiff has submitted herself to the court's jurisdiction.   Immunity protects non-resident attorneys, parties, and witnesses from being served with process in an unrelated action while in attendance or in transit to a trial, criminal or civil, within the state. It also has been extended to cover persons who were within the state for the sole purpose of discussing an out-of-court settlement.

Since the doctrine is premised on a desire to encourage non-residents to voluntarily enter the state when they otherwise could remain outside, it does not apply if the potential defendant entered the state before any action was brought but subsequently was detained involuntarily and then served with process. Similarly, the doctrine is of no utility if the person is subject to the extraterritorial long-arm jurisdiction of the court as he cannot prevent service merely by staying outside the state's borders. Thus, with the great expansion of long-arm jurisdiction in recent years, immunity from process has become a doctrine of decreasing utility for parties, although it still plays an important role for witnesses.

D. CHALLENGE TO THE PLAINTIFF'S SELECTION

1. DIRECT ATTACK

§ 2–27. Subject Matter Jurisdiction

Because issues of subject matter jurisdiction address the court's constitutional or statutory power to entertain a particular controversy, they involve questions concerning the very nature of the court itself and are not matters of personal right. Thus, an objection to subject matter jurisdiction can be made at any time throughout the proceedings; it even may be raised for the first time on appeal. Consistent with this flexibility, a party may raise this defense either in his responsive pleading or by a separate motion to dismiss (Rule 12(b)). Further, the court has an independent obligation to inquire into its subject matter jurisdiction and may raise any issues relating thereto sua sponte at the trial or appellate level. In sum, there are no real limitations on the raising of a subject matter defense during the course of the proceedings to which the objection is being made.

§ 2–28.   Personal Jurisdiction

As issues of personal jurisdiction are tied to the personal due process rights of the defendant, the defendant can waive objections to the court's power over him. Consent to jurisdiction may occur prior to any suit being filed, see § 2–15, supra. When it occurs after an action is brought, a serious problem is presented. Except in the rare circumstance in which the defendant makes a formal statement waiving all personal jurisdiction objections, it is necessary to establish some means by which the court can ascertain when the defendant has participated in the proceedings to such a degree that it would be appropriate to hold that he impliedly has waived any objections and consents to jurisdiction. The method commonly used is to establish special rules as to how defendants can object to personal jurisdiction. The failure to comply with the procedures established constitutes consent.

A common method of challenging the court's personal jurisdiction is by special appearance. Many states require a defendant who wishes to object to personal jurisdiction to enter a "special appearance" prior to answering on the merits. Typically in order to preserve this objection the defendant is not permitted to introduce any other defenses at that time or prior to making the special appearance. If he does so, he will be deemed to have made a general appearance and to have waived the right to object to jurisdiction. If the court finds that jurisdiction does not exist, the suit will be dismissed. If it rules against the defendant, then the question presented is whether the defendant waives the right to object on appeal by proceeding to defend on the merits. In states allowing appeals only from final judgments, the defendant has preserved his objection by making the initial special appearance and may raise the objection anew on a direct appeal from the final judgment on the merits. In other states that provide for some sort of interlocutory appeal, the defendant waives the objection by failing immediately to appeal the court's ruling before defending on the merits and, in that event, will not be allowed to raise the jurisdiction issue on an appeal from the final judgment. In either case, once the defendant enters a special appearance and receives an adverse ruling, the only means of obtaining further review is by a direct appeal; he cannot subsequently default and attempt to collaterally attack the judgment on personal jurisdiction grounds. See § 2–32, infra.

The distinction between general and special appearances has been abolished in the federal courts and in those states that have adopted the federal rules. Instead of requiring the defendant to make a special appearance in order to object to personal jurisdiction, the defendant may raise the objection either in a pretrial motion to dismiss or in the answer, Rule 12(b). Further, other objections may be raised at the same time. The defendant's options are circumscribed primarily by timing constraints. The failure to raise a personal jurisdiction defense in a pretrial motion when other defenses are made by motions to dismiss, Rule 12(g), or to include the defense in the answer when no pretrial motions have been made, Rule 12(h)(1), will result in the total waiver of the defense. As in the case of a special appearance, once a timely objection has been made, it may be raised again on a direct appeal, but it cannot be the basis for a collateral attack.

§ 2–29. Limited Appearances

In actions based on quasi in rem jurisdiction, special problems have arisen because of a desire to give the defendant an opportunity to protect the property seized without forcing him to submit himself to the court's in personam jurisdiction. A number of states have adopted the device of a limited appearance in response to this problem. In those states, the defendant by making a limited appearance can defend the action on the merits; if he loses only the property will be forfeited; if he wins no res judicata effect will be given to the judgment so the plaintiff may sue again in another court in which jurisdiction may be obtained. In states not utilizing this device, the defendant faced with a proper quasi in rem action has two options: (1) he can default and thereby forfeit the property, or (2) he can enter to defend on the merits and thereby submit to the court's in personam jurisdiction. Which option is preferable will depend on the value of the attached property as compared to the amount of damages being sought by the plaintiff.

The federal rules do not address the propriety of limited appearances. Thus, in actions brought in the federal courts the availability of the procedure depends on whether the court refers to state law as the governing law on that issue. See § 8–2, infra. Because courts are split on the propriety of making a limited appearance (with the slightly more prevalent view allowing it), it is most important to check the local law where the action is brought to determine its availability.

Perhaps because of the seeming wastefulness of a second trial when the first was fully litigated, a few courts have suggested that collateral estoppel effect should be given to the issues actually decided in the first quasi in rem action. However, giving even this limited binding effect to the judgment effectively treats it as in personam, to the detriment of the defendant. Thus, this approach is somewhat controversial and not uniformly agreed upon.

§ 2–30.   Venue and Service of Process

Objections to the court's venue or the means or form of service of process must be made at the outset of the action or they will be waived. This is true because both venue and service of process involve concerns of a less important nature than those present in subject matter or personal jurisdiction. Since venue restrictions are designed primarily to identify a convenient forum, the failure of the defendant to point out the lack of venue either in a pretrial motion to dismiss or in the answer will be deemed acquiescence. Indeed, in many instances the remedy for improper venue is not dismissal, but transfer, see § 2-31, infra. Service of process objections that do not involve the failure to give actual notice or to obtain personal jurisdiction present primarily technical problems dealing with the form or method of process. Thus, defects of that character are waivable unless raised by pretrial motion or in the answer. Further, although it is important to comply with the statutory requirements for service of process, the court often will not dismiss the action if the defect can be corrected by amending the process. Thus, most commonly, motions objecting to service are joined with motions to dismiss based on a lack of personal jurisdiction. When filed alone, they frequently are dilatory tactics.

§ 2-31. Forum Non Conveniens and Transfer

There are circumstances in which although the forum chosen by the plaintiff meets venue requirements, a better, more convenient forum exists. In recognition of this fact, the judicial doctrine of *forum non conveniens* developed, under which the defendant may make a motion to dismiss the action, even though the plaintiff's choice of forum meets all statutory and constitutional requirements. The motion is addressed to the court's discretion and will be granted only infrequently, typically when the plaintiff's forum is clearly inconvenient and an alternative forum exists that is a vast improvement. In several states a dismissal for forum non is not allowed whenever the plaintiff is a resident of the forum state. Further, in order to protect the plaintiff, a court granting the motion often will do so only on condition that the defendant consent to suit in the alternative forum.

In the federal court system and within several states, forum non conveniens has been codified in a transfer statute. See 28 U.S.C.A. § 1404. These statutes permit the court to transfer the case to another court within the same system where it might have been brought. Thus, the transferee forum also must meet jurisdiction and venue requirements. Unlike what occurs on a forum non motion, however, either party may move to transfer, and they need not dismiss and then recommence the action. Perhaps because of this, transfer often may be obtained on a lesser showing of inconvenience than would be neecssary if a forum non motion were presented. Nonetheless, even in those systems having transfer statutes, forum non conveniens remains an important tool as transfers are limited to courts within the same system. If the defendant wants to change from a federal forum to a state court or to a court in another country or from one state court to the state courts in another state, a motion to dismiss for forum non conveniens is the appropriate method.

One further difference between forum non conveniens and transfer should be noted. Forum non conveniens is premised on the fact that both the original court and some other court meet all the applicable jurisdiction and venue requirements. Although transfer can be only to a court in which the action could have been brought, special statutory provisions in the federal system permit transfer when the original forum had no venue to a court where venue is proper. 28 U.S.C.A. § 1406 (a). In addition, the Supreme Court has upheld a transfer when the transferor court had no personal jurisdiction and the statute of limitations had run so that to dismiss the suit for lack of jurisdiction would have resulted in forfeiting the claim. Goldlawr, Inc. v. Heiman, 369 U.S. 463 (1962). This application of the transfer statute should not be extended too easily, however, as it could result in blatant abuse and harassment by the plaintiff. Thus, it typically will be restricted to situations in which the lack of personal jurisdiction was not clear at the outset, so that dismissal would be unduly harsh to the plaintiff.

2.   COLLATERAL ATTACK

§ 2-32.   Principles Governing

If the defendant interposes an objection to the plaintiff's choice of the forum in action A in an action to enforce the judgment obtained in A or in some other proceeding, B, before another trial court, this is called a collateral attack on the judgment in A. The availability of collateral attack is severely restricted because it erodes the finality and stability of judgments. In situations in which action B is in a different court system than A it violates statutory, 28 U.S.C.A. § 1785, and constitutional principles, Art. IV, § 1, providing that full faith and credit should be given to sister state judgments. Thus, collateral attack is available only when the type of objection the defendant raises is of a constitutional dimension; venue objections being merely matters of convenience or service of process objections that involve merely the form of the service never can be raised on collateral attack.

The following rules apply to decide when a collateral attack is available as a means of raising a subject matter or personal jurisdiction defense. If the defendant never appears in action A and a default judgment is entered, then the judgment may be collaterally attacked on either ground. If the defendant appears and raises the jurisdiction objections, fully litigating them in the trial court in A, then collateral attack is barred; his only further remedy is a direct attack on appeal. If the defendant appears in A and defends on the merits, never raising any objections to personal jurisdiction, collateral attack is not available to later raise the defense. The personal jurisdiction defense was waived by the failure to make a timely objection. The problem of whether to allow collateral attack on subject matter jurisdiction grounds when the defendant has fully participated in the first proceeding, but failed to raise any objection there is more complicated since parties cannot consent to the subject matter jurisdiction of the court. Section 10 of the Restatement Second, Judgments, suggests that the court consider five factors designed to aid in balancing the conflicting policies of finality and limited jurisdiction. The few cases that have considered the problem suggest that typically collateral attack will not be available. However, if the policy against the court's acting beyond its jurisdiction is strong, as when a state court improperly hears matters confined to the exclusive jurisdiction of the federal courts, or when the jurisdictional defect raises problems of sovereign immunity, then a collateral attack may be permitted.

III. PRETRIAL: FRAMING THE LITIGATION

A. PLEADING

§ 3-1. General Theory of Pleading

The pleadings are the papers by which the litigants first set the case before the court. A thorough study of the art of pleading embraces both procedural and substantive concerns. *How* you plead is a procedural question, depending on the specific rules of the court in which you are appearing. *What* you plead is determined by considerations of substantive law and the knowledge of what facts are legally significant in each context. The primary focus in this book is on the first question. For a more detailed discussion of the art of pleading, see F. James & J. Hazard, *Civil Procedure* 55–170 (2d ed. 1977).

There have been four historic functions associated with pleading: (1) notice giving; (2) fact revelation; (3) issue formulation; and (4) screening to constrict or expand the flow of litigation in a particular court system. Different procedural systems rely on the pleadings for one or the other or a combination of these purposes. Depending on which one of these functions is emphasized, more or less detail may be required and a given pleading may be deemed sufficient or insufficient and subject to dismissal. Thus, it is important to understand the philosophy underlying the system in which you are suing in order to better understand the level of specificity or degree of flexibility that exists.

§ 3-2. History: Common Law Pleading

Although it is virtually non-existent in American courts today, common law pleading is the direct antecedent of modern code and federal rule pleading and is important to consider in order to better evaluate the present pleading rules. Pleading in common law courts was characterized by rigid formality and precision; its object was to produce through the pleadings a single issue for trial. A plaintiff could plead only a single cause of action in a given case and the defendant could make only one response. Alternative or multiple defenses were not permitted. The failure to comply with the pleading rules resulted in the dismissal of the action, with no leave to replead. Thus, the course of pleading was perilous and great attention was given to that portion of the proceedings as the pleadings truly acted as a screening device, preventing many cases from going forward. Suits in equity courts were not governed by the same rigid, complex system. Since those proceedings were solely before a judge, joinder of claims and parties was allowed, some discovery was avail-

able, and the pleadings did not act as the prime
screening device.

A brief description of common law pleading will
illustrate its formality, as well as pitfalls.   In
order to bring an action, the plaintiff had to determine which of the existing forms of action best
suited the facts of his case and obtain the proper
writ (summons) for that form of action.   Examples of the historic forms of action are detinue,
debt, replevin, covenant, trespass, and trespass on
the case.   The forms of action were essentially
categories of legal liability; if no form of action
existed to meet plaintiff's needs, there was no remedy for the alleged wrong.   The use of the wrong
writ resulted in a dismissal with prejudice.   Defense counsel were faced with a similar array of
carefully defined responses.   Defendant could: (1)
deny that the facts if true gave plaintiff a legal
right to relief (a demurrer); (2) enter a dilatory
plea challenging plaintiff's right to have the case
heard by the court before whom it was lodged;
or (3) enter a plea in bar, denying that the alleged
facts were true (a traverse) or arguing that even
if the facts were true, other facts rendered the
right unenforceable (confession and avoidance).
These alternatives were mutually exclusive, even
though they are not necessarily contradictory.   If
defendant pleaded in confession and avoidance, no
issue was joined on the facts and the plaintiff had
to respond to the newly introduced facts by demur-

rer, traverse, or another confession and avoidance.

As time pased, the common law pleading system became encrusted with requirements and risks so that actions were won or lost not on the merits, but due to pleading niceties. The desire to produce a single, clear issue for trial became outweighed by the need to develop a system more responsive to the needs of the parties and less filled with pitfalls for the unwary. These feelings underlay the development of state pleading codes and ultimately federal rule pleading.

1. PLAINTIFF

§ 3–3. The Complaint: Code Pleading

Following the lead of New York, which adopted the Field Code in 1848, several states enacted statutes to govern the procedures in their courts. The pleading requirements included in those statutes most commonly are referred to as code pleading.

Code pleading abolished the forms of action and eradicated much of the extreme formality and resulting pitfalls of common law pleading. The function of the pleadings was transformed from one of issue formulation to fact revelation. The plaintiff has only to plead the facts of a legal right and wrong—the facts showing that he possesses a right to relief. If the allegations fit into some pattern of an established right, the case can continue. Further, the plaintiff can plead alternatively and even inconsistently, at least when the facts are not all within her knowledge, as long as the pleading is in good faith. The only restraint on alternative allegations is that they must be placed in separate counts so as to give adequate notice to the defendant. Multiple causes of action may be alleged, as long as they too are placed in separate counts.

While the rigid formality of the common law has been abandoned under the codes, fact pleading presents its own high threshold for entry to the state courts, screening out cases based on vague or frivolous assertions. The level of detailed facts that must be pleaded is a question that has produced its own judicial quandary. It usually has been said that the plaintiff need plead only ultimate facts, not evidentiary facts or legal conclusions. Attempts to delineate the difference between these three terms fill the case reports. In practice, the distinction is primarily one of how much detail is involved. Thus, ultimate facts are those essential to show that the plaintiff has a cause of action. Under a theory of cause of action as the breach of a primary right, the plaintiff must allege a primary right possessed by him, a corresponding duty on the defendant and the facts showing a wrong by the defendant constituting a breach. Any special damages also must be alleged. Evidentiary facts provide greater detail and legal conclusions are necessarily more general and vague. The pleading of evidentiary facts, while improper, generally is harmless and will not result in dismissal. However, a pleading that is filled with legal conclusions may be fatally defective.

In some contract cases, code pleading states also have authorized the use of the common counts, which provide an exception to the normal degree of specificity that is required. Under the common counts the pleader need allege only that he is suing for money had and received, (quantum valebat) or for services rendered but not paid for (quantum meruit). No further facts need be alleged. Thus, in an action based on a common count, there is much less emphasis on the pleadings; indeed, so much so that the common counts remain somewhat anomalous in the code pleading system. The best explanation for the tolerance of this vague pleading standard is that the type of action involved is really one for restitution, premised on a desire to prevent the defendant from being unjustly enriched. Thus, the action is equitable in nature and historically did not fall within the common law pleading system.

§ 3–4. The Complaint: Federal ("Notice") Pleading

The most liberal pleading system is that utilized in the federal courts, and in the many state courts that have adopted the federal rules. Under the federal system, notice pleading prevails with the sole concern being whether the complaint reveals enough information so that the defendant can respond and understand why he is being sued. The standard usually suggested is that plaintiff must allege a claim showing that she is entitled to some relief. Consistent with this liberal approach, the plaintiff can plead alternatively and inconsistently, even within the same count. Fed. Rule 8(e)(2). Similarly, although the plaintiff must include a demand for relief, Fed.Rule 8(a) (3), the court is not bound by the demand in a contested case and can award whatever relief is appropriate. Fed.Rule 54(c). The ad damnum clause limits recovery only in default situations. A good illustration of the simplicity of federal pleading is the Official Forms produced by the rulemakers. See, e. g., Forms 5, 6, 8, and 11.

The primary restraint placed on plaintiffs to discourage the filing of frivolous or unsubstantiated claims is that the attorney is required to sign the pleadings attesting to the fact that the claim is filed in good faith and there is a legitimate basis for bringing the action. See Fed.Rule 11. Serious questions have been raised concerning the effectiveness of the signature requirement as a control device. There are very few cases actually imposing sanctions because of its violation. Nonetheless, it remains, at least in general actions, the main requirement imposing some constraints on the plaintiff's ability to file a complaint in federal court.

The only exception to the very liberal pleading requirements of the federal rules is in some very specific types of cases in which, by special rule, more detail is required. See Fed.Rule 9. For example, in fraud actions it is not enough to allege merely that the defendant committed a fraud. Rather, the pleader must allege the circumstances surrounding the fraud. The same is true in actions for defamation. The different treatment given to these actions undoubtedly reflects, in part, the fact that they are "disfavored" actions. Traditionally, the courts have treated these types of actions rigorously because of their potential as tools of harassment. To discourage frivolous suits in these areas, a higher pleading threshold is utilized.

The reason for the general de-emphasis on factual revelation in the federal pleading rules was the desire of the rulemakers to eliminate some of the pleading-motion practice, in which significant amounts of time and money were spent on technicalities prior to reaching the merits of the case. The burden of fact revelation is placed on the dis-

covery process (see §§ 3–19—3–31, infra), eliminating what often were definitional squabbles at
the pleading stage. Of course, one necessary effect
of liberalizing the pleading requirements is to lower the threshold for bringing an action in the
federal courts. The notice-giving philosophy of
the federal system makes an early dismissal on
the pleadings almost impossible to obtain.

§ 3–5. The Reply

In both the code and federal systems, pleadings
beyond the complaint and answer are generally
disfavored or forbidden. This development reflects the de-emphasis on pleadings in modern legal systems. In certain limited circumstances, as
when the defendant's answer contains an affirmative defense or a counterclaim, the plaintiff may
be allowed, or even required, to file a reply. However, a majority of courts do not permit a reply
to affirmative defenses, treating them as automatically denied. When a reply is filed, the plaintiff is in a defensive posture, responding to the defendant's allegations, and the general rules governing responsive pleading apply. See § 3–6, infra.
No pleadings beyond the reply are permitted.

2. DEFENDANT

§ 3–6. The Answer

The defendant has several options as to how
to respond to the plaintiff's complaint under both

the codes and the federal rules. As is discussed
in the following section, he can enter a plea in
abatement either by motion or in his answer. He
also can enter a denial, can introduce an affirmative defense, and can seek independent relief from
the plaintiff. Each of these last three options
may be used alternatively or in combination and
all should be included in the defendant's responsive pleading—the answer.

There are five different types of denials that
may be entered. Each one places in issue the matter denied. The major problem in deciding which
to utilize is that the denial must be truthful and
cannot be misleading; the defendant only can
place in issue those matters that actually are in
dispute. A *general denial* puts in issue all matters set forth in the complaint, and thus typically
cannot be utilized truthfully. Alternatively, the
defendant can enter a *specific denial,* denominating those paragraphs that are in dispute. The
failure to deny the other paragraphs results in
their admission. Similarly, a *qualified denial* may
be used, denying only specific averments within a
given paragraph. These three types of denials
are the most common. Most judicial systems also
allow the defendant to enter a denial on the ground
that he has *insufficient knowledge to form a belief* as to the truth or falsity of a given allegation
in the complaint. This form of denial must be
used with caution. The issue must be one out-

side the defendant's knowledge and, further, one about which the defendant could not easily have informed himself. It is unclear exactly what burden is placed on the defendant to gain the requisite knowledge and the court will decide on a case by case basis whether that defense is legitimate. If the denial is found inappropriate, the matter which was so denied will be deemed admitted. The last form of denial that may be utilized is a *denial on information and belief.* This approach is used most often by corporate defendants who are being sued because of the activities of some of their employees. It is permitted because the information available to the corporation at the time of filing the answer may be only second-hand. This denial allows them to protect themselves should later information reveal the truth of the plaintiff's allegations.

In addition to pleading some form of denial, the defendant may include an affirmative defense in the answer. Affirmative defenses are descendants of the common law plea in confession and avoidance: the defendant admits the truth of plaintiff's allegation, but alleges new facts that should require the dismissal of the action. Unlike the common law, however, affirmative defenses may be used in conjunction with denials. The defendant in admitting the plaintiff's allegations does so only for purposes of the defense. Examples of affirmative defenses are statute of limitations, res judicata, assumption of the risk, and release. Any defense that seeks to avoid the plaintiff's allegations by introducing new facts, rather than attempting to destroy the allegations in the complaint may be deemed an affirmative defense. This definition is an important one to understand; the failure to include an affirmative defense in the answer usually will result in its waiver. The rationale for this rule is that since the defense introduces new facts, its omission from the pleadings fails to notify the plaintiff so that it would be unfair to allow its assertion at a later time. While the courts sometimes will allow amendments to raise these defenses, see §§ 3–8— 3–9, infra, the ability to amend is a limited one. Thus, a good rule of thumb is: when in doubt as to whether a given defense is affirmative, plead it.

The final matter to consider including in the answer is a request for some affirmative or independent relief from the plaintiff. This is referred to either as a counterclaim or cross-complaint. The rules regarding when a defendant is permitted to seek affirmative relief in this manner are discussed elsewhere, see § 3–19, infra. For pleading purposes, a defendant in this position is treated like a claimant and the same pleading requirements that govern the complaint control the assertion of a claim in the answer.

3.   CHALLENGES TO THE PLEADINGS

§ 3–7.   Methods of Challenging the Pleadings

There are a wide range of challenges that may be made to the pleadings.   Most commonly, the challenges are made by the defendant who seeks to dismiss or delay the action on grounds unrelated to the merits.   The possibility of interposing an objection primarily to delay the time when a responsive pleading must be filed has resulted in these types of objections being referred to as dilatory pleas.   However, the plaintiff also may attempt to challenge the defendant's pleadings.

The types of challenges that may be made are the same in code pleading and federal rule jurisdictions.   The major difference between the two systems is in form.   Objections to the pleadings in code states are made either by a motion to quash or by general or special demurrer, whereas objections under the federal rules are made by a specifically denominated motion or they may be included in the responsive pleading.

In general, the kinds of challenges available can be divided into three categories.   In the first category, the defendant may object to the court's power to entertain the action, i. e. objections to personal and subject matter jurisdiction and venue, or to some defect in parties.   In the second category, the defendant's challenge is to the complaint itself. By general demurrer or a motion to dismiss under Federal Rule 12(b)(6), the defendant can argue that the plaintiff has failed to state a claim for relief or a cause of action. This challenge can be directed to the entire complaint or to only some counts in the complaint. Further, it points only to defects on the face of the complaint: the plaintiff actually may possess a claim, he simply has not properly pleaded one. Thus, most often dismissals on this ground are with leave to amend and the demurrer or motion acts merely to search the record. Both of these types of challenges are directed toward claims for relief rather than defenses and consequently are utilized most frequently by defendants. However, when the defendant has included a claim for relief in the answer, the plaintiff may raise either challenge just described.

The third type of challenge that may be made also is based on pleading defects. The object is not to obtain a dismissal, but is to cure alleged deficiencies in the pleadings. Either a plaintiff or a defendant may make a motion to strike specific paragraphs or sentences. Objections operating as the basis for a motion to strike may challenge matter that is redundant or immaterial or that which is sham or scandalous. The motion to strike acts to prune the pleadings and generally is disfavored, given the great de-emphasis on the pleadings in modern litigation. In addition to a motion to strike, the defendant can question any matter that is ambiguous, unintelligible or generally uncertain in the complaint by special demurrer or by a motion for a more definite statement. This challenge cannot be used merely as a fishing device and is only available to a party who is required to file a responsive pleading. Given the few situations in which the plaintiff is allowed to file a reply (see § 3–5, supra), this objection is one made most typically by defendants. The general standard used by the courts in deciding whether to grant these motions is whether the defects are such that the defendant cannot respond adequately unless a more definite statement is made. If a responsive pleading could be made without any additional information, then the challenge will be overruled and the defendant must rely on discovery to flesh out or clarify the case further.

B.   AMENDMENTS

§ 3–8.   General Standards and Practice

At common law the pleadings assumed a dominant and controlling role and thus, concomitantly, the ability to amend was virtually nonexistent. No variance was tolerated between the pleadings and the proof at trial and a departure in the evidence from the issue as framed in the pleadings led to the dismissal of the suit. Modern code and federal practice differs radically from this approach. Amendments to the pleadings are allowed quite liberally in an effort to decide cases on their merits, rather than on technicalities, and variance between the pleadings and the proof is permissible. Amendments have been allowed at trial and even after judgment in an effort to render justice. Further, if evidence is introduced at trial on an issue not raised in the pleadings and no objection is raised, the court may deem the pleadings amended by the implied consent of the opposing party. See Fed.Rule 15(b). The overriding concern is to reach the merits, but not prejudice or mislead the opposing party because of a failure to include an issue or theory at the pleading stage.

§ 3–9. Statutes of Limitation: Relation Back

The most difficult problem involving amendments arises when a proposed amendment seeks to add a new claim or party after the statute of limitations has run. This problem commonly is described in terms of whether the amendment will be allowed to relate back to the institution of the action. The problem is really one of notice: did the opposing party have notice within the statutory period that this new claim would be asserted. If not, the amendment should not be allowed to relate back.

The notice issue is handled somewhat differently depending on whether the amendment proposes
to add a new claim between the already existing
parties or seeks to add new parties themselves.
In the first situation, the amendment typically
will be allowed if the new facts or theories being
alleged are part of the same cause of action (code
states) or arise out of the same transaction or
occurrence (federal rules practice) as presented in
the original pleadings. This standard is designed
to assure that the new claim bears a close relationship with the claims already in the action. Notice
then is presumed because of the close relationship
of the amendment to the original pleadings.

The addition of new parties does not allow the
same presumption. Thus, under the federal rules
not only must the amendment present a transactionally related claim, but also the court must be
able to find that the new party received some notice of the claim before the statute of limitations
ran and knew that, but for a mistake he should
have been a named party. See Fed.Rule 15(c).
Practice in code pleading states is somewhat more
ambiguous. There is no separate test for amendments adding parties; the cause of action test governs all amendments. Typically, the presence of a
new party means that there is a new cause of action because different rights and duties are at issue. Thus, party amendments are strictly limited.
In some states, such as California, John Doe com-

plaints are allowed and an issue arises as to whether the substitution of a real party for the fictitious one can be accomplished through an amendment relating back to the filing of the complaint. The courts have interpreted cause of action in these circumstances to mean the same facts, which would appear to allow unlimited amendments to substitute actual persons for John Does. However, recent authority suggests that the court will look carefully at the complaint to make certain that the claim being asserted against the newly named party was clearly stated and contemplated in the original complaint. Totally new claims against new parties cannot be accomplished by using the John Doe device, even though they arise out of the same facts. Marasco v. Wadsworth, 139 Cal.Rptr. 143 (1977). If the claim was clearly within the scope of the complaint, the amendment will be allowed even though there was no actual notice to those parties.

C. JOINDER OF PARTIES AND CLAIMS

1. PARTY JOINDER

§ 3–10. Parties Who Must be Joined

Although generally the plaintiff decides where, when and whom to sue, the plaintiff is not given complete freedom. Rules denominating who are real parties in interest and who are necessary or indispensable parties to the action place some limitations on the plaintiff.   See §§ 3–11—3–12, infra.

The rules governing who must be joined serve several important functions. As the name suggests, real party in interest rules assure that the named plaintiff is the person who possesses the substantive right being sued upon. If the suit is not brought by a real party in interest, it may be dismissed unless a proper plaintiff can be joined. In this way, the defendant is protected from potentially harassing and duplicative litigation. Historically, the rule provided a means of identifying the actual owner of a right when there had been an assignment or some other transfer in interest prior to the action. In modern times, the rule simply clarifies who is a proper party plaintiff.

In the federal courts the real party in interest rule also denominates the persons whose citizenship controls for purposes of diversity jurisdiction. This latter function of the rule poses some problems in cases in which it is alleged that a non-resident administrator was appointed or an assignment was made so as to create or destroy federal diversity jurisdiction. Viewed as a device to create diversity, such a transfer in interest may be held to violate the federal statute forbidding the collusive creation of jurisdiction. 28 U.S.C.A. § 1359. Nonetheless, the transfer may be valid under state law. The Supreme Court has struck down an assignment of interest solely for collection purposes that was accomplished so as to create diversity. Kramer v. Caribbean Mills, Inc., 394 U.S. 823 (1969). Conversely, it has ruled that assignments of interest or appointments of representatives made to defeat diversity are not prohibited by any existing federal statute. Mecom v. Fitzsimmons Drilling Co., 284 U.S. 183 (1931). In the case of the appointment of a non-resident administrator to create diversity jurisdiction, the lower courts have split on whether it is proper to consider the motive behind the appointment. In an effort to avoid this problem the American Law Institute has proposed that the representative party, though he is a real party in interest, be treated as having the same citizenship as the person being represented. ALI, Study of the Division of Jurisdiction Between State and Federal Courts, Official Draft, § 1301(b)(4) (1969).

The necessary and indispensable party rules compel party joinder in order to protect persons who might be harmed by a judgment entered in their absence or, conversely, to protect existing parties who might not be able to obtain complete relief without the presence of those absent persons. The focus is on the impact of the judgment if those persons are not joined. The difference between a necessary and an indispensable party has posed some problems for the courts. See §

3–12, infra. Nonetheless, the rules serve the important function of protecting existing parties, as well as absent persons, from piecemeal or harmful litigation.

§ 3–11. Real Parties in Interest and Capacity to Sue

Real party in interest rules should be distinguished from rules governing a party's capacity to sue or be sued. As just described above, the former attempt to assure that the named plaintiff possesses the substantive right on which the suit is based. Capacity rules stipulate whether a party is qualified to appear as a named party in an action. They are dependent upon the character of the parties, not the rights involved. Typically, rules denying legal capacity are designed to protect certain classes of persons who might not be able to adequately protect their own interests. Criteria such as age and mental ability often determine a person's capacity to sue. For example, a minor child who is harmed in an automobile accident has no capacity to sue, although she does possess a cause of action. Her guardian or parents also will be deemed real parties in interest and, having capacity, may sue for her. Because capacity rules focus on the abilities of certain classes of persons, rather than the question whether they possess a claim for relief, they apply both to plaintiffs and defendants.

§ 3–12. Necessary and Indispensable Parties

The question whether a party is necessary or indispensable to a particular law suit turns largely on the degree or directness of his interest in the action. The principle supporting the compulsory joinder of these persons is an equitable one—an attempt to assure that any judgment entered will do justice for all concerned. Necessary parties may be defined as persons who have an interest in the litigation and whose interest might *possibly* be affected by a judgment entered in their absence. Indispensable parties possess interests that would *inevitably* be affected by any decree in the suit. Any person who is found to be either necessary or indispensable should be joined. In some cases, however, joinder may be impossible because the person may not be within the personal jurisdictional reach of the court. In the federal courts, joinder also may be prevented because the presence of the new party would destroy diversity of citizenship, the court's subject matter jurisdiction. In either situation, the question whether the party is necessary or indispensable is crucial. If he is merely necessary, the suit may proceed in his absence. If he is indispensable, it must be dismissed. Because of the serious effects of a finding of indispensability, courts evaluating this question will look carefully to see whether the decree can be shaped in such a way to avoid inevitably affecting the absentee's interest or to grant some relief

[*97*]

to the existing parties in his absence. If so, then the party will be found to be only necessary and the suit need not be dismissed.

In the federal system the rulemakers in 1966 abandoned the terminology and approach of deciding the question who must be joined in terms of who is a necessary or indispensable party. Rather than focusing on categories of parties, the federal practice requires the court to consider specific pragmatic factors in order to balance the equities of the situation and reach a decision. The United States Supreme Court interpreted the federal joinder provision, Fed.Rule 19, in Provident Tradesmens Bank & Trust Co. v. Lumbermens Mut. Cas. Co., 390 U.S. 102 (1968). The Court suggested the following approach to compulsory joinder questions. Once it is determined that the absent person has an interest in the litigation that might practically be impaired by a decree in his absence or that might prevent the existing parties to the suit from obtaining complete relief, that person is a Rule 19(a) party and should be joined. If he cannot be, Rule 19(b) sets out four factors for the court to consider and balance in deciding whether to dismiss or proceed. First, it should consider the plaintiff's interest in the forum and whether another forum might accommodate better all the interested parties. Second, it should determine whether the failure to dismiss will subject the defendant to multiple litigation. Third, the interest of the absent person should be examined carefully to see whether it will be foreclosed as a practical matter by the judgment or if there is some way of shaping the relief or staying the execution on the judgment in order to protect his interest. Fourth, the court should consider the issue of judicial economy and whether the present action represents an efficient means of settling the controversy. Although the Supreme Court did not explain what weight to give each of the four factors, it did suggest that the trial courts should attempt to apply Rule 19(b) in such a way as to avoid dismissal unless it is absolutely necessary. If the person should intervene in the action, none of these concerns need be addressed.

The equitable concerns behind the compulsory party joinder rule are so important that the failure to join an indispensable or Rule 19(b) party may be raised by the court on its own motion, or it may be raised on appeal even though the issue never was addressed at trial. Thus, several courts have characterized this defect in parties as constituting a lack of subject matter jurisdiction. The defect is not jurisdictional, but equitable, and it cannot be used to collaterally attack an otherwise valid judgment.

§ 3–13. Parties Who May be Joined

Various rules exist governing who may be joined by the plaintiff in a lawsuit, who may be added to the lawsuit by the defendant or who may enter a lawsuit of their own volition. The addition of these parties to the action is restricted by rule requirements, as well as by general jurisdictional restraints. The court must be able to assert personal jurisdiction over each of the parties in the suit and, in the federal courts, subject matter jurisdiction must be established over each of the claims between the various parties. The rules authorizing party joinder do not alter or affect the court's jurisdictional powers. The following sections will explore the restraints imposed by the rules on party joinder.

§ 3–14. Proper Parties

The term proper parties refers to those persons whom the plaintiff may join as parties to an action when it is commenced. The joinder of a proper party is totally permissive so that the failure to join an otherwise proper party will not result in the dismissal of the suit. Under most code systems, which follow the equity practice, any person who has an interest in the subject matter of the suit or the relief may be joined in the action. A few state courts interpret this requirement liberally and literally, encouraging joinder. However, most courts under the early codes ruled that any person joined must have an interest in all the relief being sought.   Under this restrictive interpretation, a husband and wife could not join as plaintiffs in a suit arising out of a car accident if they each were asserting personal injury claims. In that event neither plaintiff would have a legal interest in the personal injury recovery of the other.

Under modern joinder practice, as exemplified by the federal rules, the joinder of proper parties is determined by a standard designed to promote judicial economy and prevent the action from becoming unwieldy or cluttered with unrelated parties and claims.   If the claims for relief by or against the persons sought to be joined arise out of the same transaction or occurrence or series thereof and if the joined parties share *any* common question of law or fact, then joinder is proper. See Fed.Rule 20.   The issue of what constitutes a transaction is within the court's discretion and it frequently depends upon the predominance of common questions.   The greater the overlap in evidence, the more efficiency that will be gained by allowing joinder.   In the case of defendant joinder, the courts also may be inclined to construe transaction broadly because to disallow joinder may produce inconsistent verdicts and ultimately leave the plaintiff remediless.

§ 3–15. Impleaded Parties (Third-Party Defendants)

In order to provide defending parties an opportunity to more fully protect themselves, most procedural systems provide some mechanism by which the defendant can bring in (implead), a third-party defendant. See Fed.Rule 14. The two requirements for impleader are that the person is not already a party to the action and that the person "is or may be liable" to the defendant if the defendant is found liable to the original plaintiff. Thus, the most common theories for impleader are that the third-party defendant has a duty to indemnify the defendant or to contribute to the payment of plaintiff's damages. It is irrelevant that the impleaded party is directly liable to the plaintiff; he must have some legal liability towards the defendant. In the absence of impleader, the defendant would have to wait to file suit until after he had lost the main action. Impleader avoids this time lag between judgments and, because all the issues are decided in one action, it increases the likelihood of consistent results.

Once the third-party defendant is properly before the court, he is allowed to assert not only his defenses to the impleader claim, but also defenses to the main action that the original defendant may have omitted. Personal defenses, such as a lack of personal jurisdiction, may not be asserted on behalf of the original defendant. By allowing the third-party defendant to assert defenses to the main action, he can protect himself from liability should the original defendant be lax in his defense. Subject to jurisdictional limitations, the third-party defendant also may assert any claims he possesses against any of the parties to the action. Conversely, the other parties to the suit can assert additional claims directly against the impleaded defendant if they meet the jurisdictional requirements. This free assertion of claims between the parties is permitted in order to decide the entire dispute in a single action, thereby promoting judicial economy.

The decision whether to permit the impleader claim, as well as the filing of any additional claims is left to the court's discretion. The court will determine whether the joinder of this additional party or of the other claims will unduly complicate the action, improperly delay the determination of the main claim to the detriment of the original plaintiff, or confuse the jury. If so, joinder may be refused even though the claims fall within the applicable rule's requirements.

§ 3–16. Other Additional Parties

The assertion of a proper counterclaim or cross-claim between the existing parties to an action, see § 3–19, infra, may prompt the addition of another party whose presence would further the adjudication of that claim. In some instances the party may be deemed indispensable to an adjudication of the new claim so that joinder will be ordered or the claim will be dismissed, see § 3–12, supra. Other parties who have lesser interests also may be joined, as long as they meet the standard of proper parties, see § 3–14, supra. When testing the propriety of their joinder, the court will look at the relationship or interest of the additional parties in the counterclaim or cross-claim involved, rather than their relationship to the main action.

§ 3–17. Intervenors

An intervenor is a person who is not already a party to an ongoing action but who seeks to be made a party, typically because she shares some interest in the litigation and is concerned that in her absence that interest will not be adequately protected. The decision whether to allow intervention is based on a balancing of the needs or interests of the intervenor against the possible burdens on the existing parties if intervention is permitted. The court will consider whether the intervenor shares common issues with the parties; the more the intervenor is attempting to inject new issues, the greater the potential prejudice and delay to the original action. An intervenor need not argue that she will be prejudiced because she will be bound by the judgment if not joined. Intervention is permissible if she can show that her interest will be impaired as a practical matter. The timeliness of a motion to intervene also is important because the greater the delay by the intervenor, the greater the likelihood of prejudice to the existing parties.

In the federal courts the rules provide for intervention as of right, Fed.Rule 24(a), and permissive intervention, Fed.Rule 24(b). Under the former provision, if the intervenor demonstrates an interest in the action that might be impaired if intervention is not allowed, and the opposing parties do not show that that interest is already adequately represented, intervention will be allowed. Although the courts obviously have considerable leeway in deciding what constitutes a sufficient interest or whether the interest is already protected, their discretion is not boundless. Once the standard is met, intervention cannot be denied simply because it would delay the action or prejudice the existing parties. The premise for permissive intervention is merely that common questions exist and the court is given complete discretion to deny intervention despite a finding that the rule requirements are met. Although timeliness may be taken into account for intervention under both Fed.Rule 24(a) and Fed.Rule 24(b), the courts are much more inclined to grant a late motion to intervene as of right than one for permissive intervention. The difference between permissive intervention and intervention as of right also is important in the federal courts in other contexts. It affects jurisdiction (the latter claims are within the ancillary jurisdiction of the court), and appealability (orders denying intervention as of right may be appealed immediately).

2.   CLAIM JOINDER

§ 3–18.   Plaintiff Claims Joinder

The ability of the plaintiff to join several claims in one suit depends upon rules authorizing joinder and whether the claims are within the court's jurisdictional power. This latter prerequisite is important primarily in the federal courts as they have only limited jurisdiction and the application of a joinder rule cannot operate to extend their power. In the state courts the primary concern is whether joinder is authorized under the procedural rules governing the judicial system where suit is brought.

The rules governing joinder of claims by the plaintiff fall into three categories. The first is derived from the Field Code and lists a series of categories, permitting the plaintiff to join any claims that fall into a single category. See, e. g., Cal.Civ.Proc.Code § 427. In all but one category, claims are joined by subject matter (i. e., injury to the person, injury to property, contracts). In the remaining category, joinder is permitted because of a unity of occurrence—claims "arising out of the same transaction or transactions connected with the same subject of the action." Further restrictions in code pleading systems that the claims joined must affect all the parties to a dispute and must present consistent, not alternative, theories of recovery prevent joinder from being too broad. The misjoinder of claims may be challenged by demurrer and the suit dismissed until properly pleaded.

The second type of plaintiff joinder rule places no limitations on the plaintiff. See, e. g., Fed. Rule 18(a). Plaintiff is permitted to join as many claims, related or unrelated, as she may have against the defendant. Concerns about potential prejudice due to jury confusion or the convenience of trying all the claims in one suit are decided at the trial stage, when the court may order a severance of one or more of the claims for a separate trial. Misjoinder under these rules is impossible at the pleading stage.

The third type of joinder provision allows the plaintiff the same freedom to join unrelated claims, but includes a compulsory joinder provision, requiring plaintiff to join all claims arising out of the same transaction or occurrence. See, e. g., Mich.Gen.Ct.R. 203. In this way judicial economy is assured and the defendant is protected against a series of potentially harassing suits. Notably, although both of the other approaches

[*107*]

speak only of permissive joinder, the plaintiff's options under any system may be restricted by the judicial doctrines of res judicata and collateral estoppel, see §§ 6-5—6-14, infra. The potential application of those doctrines to prevent a second or third action should create some compulsion on the plaintiff to join all related claims in one action. The inclusion of a compulsory joinder provision in the rule itself makes clearer to the plaintiff the hazards of failing to join those claims and also makes easier the second court's inquiry as to whether a subsequent action should be barred.

§ 3–19. Defendant Joinder: Counterclaims and Cross-Claims

The constraints placed upon the defendant's freedom to assert and to join claims stem both from rule and jurisdictional limitations. Thus, even though the joinder of defendant's claims may be permissible under the rules, each new claim also must have some jurisdictional basis. Before considering the rule requirements, a few terminological remarks are necessary. In some states all claims asserted by a defendant are denominated "cross-complaints." Other states, as well as the federal courts, distinguish between claims asserted against opposing parties ("counterclaims") and claims between co-parties ("cross-claims"). Different limitations are placed on the defendant in each of these two situations. Thus, the lawyer

[*108*]

is advised to be careful to distinguish between cross-complaints and cross-claims as the latter is a term of art referring only to a very specific situation.

There are three questions to address when considering the propriety of defendant claims joinder. The first is what claims the defendant has the power to assert against the other parties to the action. The second question is whether the defendant can join additional claims to those specifically authorized under the rules. The third is whether the defendant can join additional parties against whom he wishes to assert a claim. It is the first question that will be addressed in this section. The defendant's ability to join additional claims is governed by the same rules and principles applicable to plaintiff claim joinder, see § 3–18, supra. The addition of parties to the action is discussed in §§ 3–15—3–16, supra.

All judicial systems permit the defendant, as a matter of rule practice, to assert any claims he may have against the opposing party, the plaintiff. The modern day counterclaim traces its roots to the historic practice of recoupment and set-off. Recoupment allowed the defendant to reduce plaintiff's recovery by proving a transactionally related claim. Set-off permitted the defendant to assert unrelated, liquidated claims against the plaintiff. In either case, no affirmative relief beyond the plaintiff's claim was allowed and the defendant

[*109*]

waived his right to claim any excess in a subsequent action.

Most modern judicial systems have a rule requiring the defendant to assert any claims that are related to the plaintiff's action, see, e. g., Fed.Rule 13(a). The failure to interpose a compulsory counterclaim will prevent the defendant from raising that claim in a separate action due to notions of waiver or estoppel. The general standard determining whether a counterclaim is compulsory is whether the claim arises out of the same transaction or occurrence as the main action. This standard generally will be met if there is a logical relationship between the claims, such as if they arise out of the same event, or if some of the same evidence must be used to prove both claims. There are a few exceptions to the compulsory counterclaim rules that act to protect the defendant from being under too great a burden. Thus, the defendant must assert only those transactionally related claims that are mature when the original complaint was served, that are not already the subject of pending litigation, and that do not require the presence of other parties over whom the court may not have jurisdiction. See Fed.Rule 13(a). Other rule provisions allow amendments prior to judgment to include omitted or newly discovered counterclaims, see, e. g., Fed.Rules 13(e), (f). Additional exceptions have been created by the courts in order to protect further the defendant. For example, if the defendant has two separate actions pending against him and his counterclaim is transactionally related to both, he may choose in which action to assert the counterclaim and need not file it in the first proceeding that was brought. Of course, if the defendant wishes to assert any of these excepted counterclaims he may do so.

Although a few states provide for the unrestricted joinder of cross-claims, see, e. g., N.Y. C.P.L. & R. 3019(b), the ability of a defendant to assert claims against co-defendants typically is much more severely limited than his ability to claim against an opposing party. In general, only cross-claims that are transactionally related to the main action are permitted under the rules, see Fed. Rule 13(g). This difference in treatment reflects a concern that the litigation of claims not directly involving the plaintiff may delay plaintiff's action and, to the extent it complicates the litigation, may prejudice the original suit. It also recognizes that complete justice between the plaintiff and the defendants can be accomplished without the adjudication of any cross-claims, whereas complete justice may not be achieved without adjudicating counterclaims. Thus, cross-claims are always permissive; the defendant may assert his claim against a co-defendant in an independent action without any risk of estoppel.

[*111*]

Although cross-claims, like compulsory counter-claims, are defined under a transaction test, there is greater disagreement among the courts as to what constitutes the same transaction for cross-claim purposes.   This difficulty in defining the transaction reflects the fact that cross-claims bring into play two conflicting concerns.   Some courts emphasize the desire to decide an entire dispute in one action, even though it involves a series of claims between different parties.   They define the transaction very broadly.   A good example of this broad joinder philosophy is a dispute arising out of a large construction project, involving claims of breach of contract between the contractors, subcontractors, architects, and the sureties.   Other courts are concerned about unnecessarily complicating and delaying the plaintiff's action and, in order to protect against that happening, interpret transaction narrowly to include only claims in which the rights of the plaintiff are involved in some way.

D. DISCOVERY

1. IN GENERAL

§ 3–20. General Principles Governing

The discovery phase of litigation serves several important purposes: it can be used to preserve evidence of witnesses who may not be available at the

time of the trial; to reveal facts; to aid in formu-
lating the issues; and to freeze testimony so as to
prevent perjury. Discovery may serve to prepare
a case for summary judgment as the parties discover that the only issues in contention are those
of law. It also may promote settlements insofar
as the parties are able by careful inquiry to test
the strength of their opponent's case. Even if it
does not result in obviating the need for a trial,
discovery, if properly utilized, should aid in producing a crystallized trial. With full revelation of
facts between the parties, the trial becomes less of
a "game of wits" and more of a probing into the
actual truth of certain facts. This results in a
systems savings, as well as a fairer or more just
trial. Thus, it is not surprising that the federal
courts and many of the states have provided for
very liberal discovery. Indeed, at present, there
are virtually no limitations on the number or types
of discovery devices that may be utilized in a
single case.

The effectiveness of any discovery system depends in great measure on whether it can operate
extrajudicially. Otherwise, the amount of time
saved at trial is lost in litigation over discovery
orders. In recognition of this fact, under the federal discovery rules, as well as in several states,
the only time the parties appear before the court
during discovery is when some problem or dis-

agreement arises concerning the valid scope of an inquiry.

This trend toward broad discovery is tied to the move away from special or rigid pleading rules. It represents a shift in the time at which a party must be able to prove his case. Notice pleading coupled with liberal discovery allows the parties to build their cases up to the point of trial, or at least summary judgment. Systems maintaining more rigid pleading rules also limit discovery and typically permit it only with tight court supervision. The parties are required to know more and be able to show more about their case at the time suit is filed or they will not be allowed into court. Obviously these two approaches represent very different philosophies. For our purposes it is not necessary to resolve which is the better approach, but only to be aware of how and why discovery operates as it does.

The discussion that follows will describe the various types of discovery devices available, using the federal system as the model. The federal procedures have been adopted in whole or in part in most of the states. However, the reader should be careful to check the specific rules of the jurisdiction in which suit is brought, as the amount of freedom in this area may vary somewhat from forum to forum.

2. DISCOVERY DEVICES: THE MECHANICS AND TACTICS

§ 3–21. Depositions

Depositions are probably the most useful and most costly of discovery devices. They can be taken of a party or a witness. A deposition acts as a sort of minitrial. The person deposed (deponent) appears before a court officer and gives sworn testimony in response to questions by the attorneys from both sides of the case. The scope of the examination is not limited by the rules of evidence; the attorneys may inquire of anything relevant, as long as it is not privileged. Examination and cross-examination occurs with the opportunity to pursue new lines of inquiry as new facts are revealed and to test the deponent as a witness, not only as to the probable substance of the testimony, but also as to demeanor, quickness, confidence, etc. The testimony then is transcribed, signed and sworn to.

While depositions may be taken anytime after an action is commenced, most rules provide that the plaintiff cannot begin a deposition until some time after the defendant is served with process, usually twenty to thirty days. This allows the defendant to obtain a lawyer and ready the case so as to be prepared at the deposition. The one exception to this restriction is special provisions authorizing a deposition to be taken even before suit is filed. See, e. g., Fed.Rule 27. This procedure is available to perpetuate the testimony of persons who most likely will not be available at trial. It only can be invoked when the requesting party states why the action has not been or cannot be filed first.

The adversarial nature of the deposition permits its use at trial for a variety of purposes. It can be used to impeach a witness whose testimony at trial varies from that of the deposition. It can be used for witnesses who are dead or outside the court's subpoena power at the time of trial. In the federal system, depositions can be introduced for witnesses more than 100 miles from the place of trial, see Fed.Rule 32(a)(3)(B). This willingness to allow "paper witnesses" because of inconvenience alone illustrates the strength of the deposition.

In many ways, the major drawback to depositions in their cost. Attorneys' fees for both sides, witness' fees, stenographers' fees and transcription costs can be extremely expensive, if not prohibitive. Further, while a party may be deposed wherever the trial is lodged, a non-party can be commanded to appear there only if she is within the subpoena power of the court. See Fed.Rule 45(d). If a deposition is desired of a distant witness, the parties and their attorneys typically must travel there, adding travel and subsistence costs to this already expensive procedure.

§ 3–22. Depositions Upon Written Questions

The major difference between depositions and depositions upon written questions is that the latter are scripted in advance. The scope of the examination in terms of who may be deposed and what information may be sought remains the same. Similarly, depositions upon written questions are governed by the same rules as general depositions regarding their use at trial.

The side requesting this procedure sends a proposed list of questions to the opposing counsel, who in turn submits a series of cross-examination questions. Redirect and recross questions also may be exchanged. The deponent then appears before the court reporter and responds to this set of prepared questions, with all answers being transcribed, signed, and sworn to.

The chief advantage of this procedure is that it is less costly than a deposition, particularly when dealing with a distant witness. Because the proceeding is limited to questions submitted in advance, none of the attorneys need be present and, by definition, the procedure takes place wherever the deponent is located. Further, as the testimony is delayed until questions are exchanged, there is no fear of the defendant being unprepared, and the procedure can be used by either party immediately after commencement of the action. However, the loss in spontaneity and flexibility in regard to what questions are asked suggests that it should never be used when deposing a hostile or key witness or when the subject under examination is very complicated. Not surprisingly, this device is not often utilized.

§ 3–23. Interrogatories

Interrogatories consist of a series of written questions to which written answers are prepared and signed under oath. They differ from depositions on written questions in that they may be directed only to parties, not witnesses, and the answers may be composed by the party and his attorney. Further, although technically the scope of proper inquiry is the same—relevant, but not privileged information—the requestor is not limited to things within the party's personal knowledge. Facts may be solicited that require the party to search his records in order to answer. The respondent has no duty, however, to investigate into matters outside his direct control. Thus, interrogatories are most useful to discover some organizational knowledge, which would require searching corporate records. They are the least expensive means of obtaining information; no burden or cost, except phrasing the questions, typically is placed on the requesting party. Further, they may be utilized at any time—even served with the summons and complaint—and are not limited as to the number that can be served.

Interrogatories usually are not used as evidence at trial. Their admissibility depends on the rules of evidence in the trial court and this means, because of the hearsay and best evidence rules, that they typically will be excluded. Thus, the primary use of interrogatories is as a start-up device. Based on the facts revealed in the answers to the interrogatories, the attorney better can determine what issues are presented and how to frame a deposition.

It should be apparent that interrogatories can be terribly burdensome and subject to considerable abuse. This is one reason why they are limited to parties. In an effort to curtail some of these abuses in the corporate context, the federal rules and several states have provisions designed to allow corporations to shift some of the burden back onto the requesting party. The corporation under these provisions can designate the records in which the answer to the interrogatories can be found and the requesting party then must search out the answer, see Fed.Rule 33(c).

§ 3–24. Discovery of Documents and Things

Document discovery refers to the means by which parties can obtain access to documents and other items not in their possession. The requesting party seeks to inspect files or examine premises or other things in order to arrive at his own conclusions regarding the facts, rather than to propound interrogatories requiring the opponents to prepare answers after reviewing their own records. The party seeking discovery may make copies of those documents of interest, take photographs, or make whatever record is appropriate.

Modern discovery rules generally provide for document discovery between the parties as soon as the action is commenced. No court order is needed. The requesting party simply asks the opponent for access to the documents or things that she wishes to investigate. Any document that is relevant, not privileged, and within the possession or control of a party may be discovered. The question of what documents are within the control of a party has posed some problems. Control clearly does not mean legal control. If a party is in a position to influence the person or organization possessing the documents, he will be deemed to control them. In the one case to reach the United States Supreme Court on this issue, Societe Internationale v. Rogers, 357 U.S. 197 (1958), the Court ruled that the defendant would have to deliver documents to the plaintiff even though under Swiss law the revelation of those documents could result in a criminal penalty! The party had the ability to influence the Swiss government to change the law or to create an exception to it and thus had control over the documents.

Non-parties also may be subject to document discovery under the subpoena power of the court. Court control over this type of discovery from witnesses assures that it will not be too burdensome or intrusive—a charge frequently labelled at party discovery. Further, in the case of non-parties, the court may impose some cost-sharing on the requesting party, see, Fed.Rule 45(b).

§ 3–25. Physical and Mental Examinations

The one discovery device that remains under the complete control of the court is requests for the physical or mental examination of parties. This discovery device has resisted constitutional attack and challenges that it violates the doctor-patient privilege, Sibbach v. Wilson, 312 U.S. 1 (1941). However, its use is strictly limited to parties or persons under the custody or legal control of parties and to situations in which the need for information outweighs the right to privacy of the person being examined.

A court will order a physical or mental exam only upon a showing that the party's health is an actual issue in controversy in the case and that there is "good cause" for granting the request. Good cause under these circumstances means more than relevance. The requesting party must show why the information is necessary and that it cannot be obtained otherwise. There must be some basis for believing that the party is suffering from some relevant physical or mental disability. Further, although it now is settled that this discovery device may be utilized against both plaintiffs and defendants, the court may be more stringent in applying the "good cause" requirement when defendants are being examined. This distinction reflects an awareness that by and large it is the plaintiff who shapes the controversy and thus easily could place the defendant's health in controversy. Despite these concerns, it is fair to say that in personal injury litigation today requests for physical and mental examinations are granted rather routinely. It is only in other litigation areas that these requests pose difficulties.

In recognition of the intrusion a court ordered examination may represent, the rules provide some reciprocal privileges to the examinee. Upon request, the person examined must be given a copy of the doctor's report. This opportunity contrasts sharply with the generally more limited access allowed to expert witnesses, see § 3–30, infra. However, if such a request is made, the opposing party then may obtain a copy of any similar reports by doctors retained by the examinee. By making the initial request, the examinee has waived the doctor-patient privilege.

§ 3–26. Admissions

Admissions are a discovery device designed to frame the issues or facts actually in controversy.

An admission obtained during discovery will establish conclusively that issue at trial, unless the court allows its later amendment or withdrawal —a very uncommon practice. It will not control in any other lawsuit. Admissions are limited to parties and essentially operate by means of an exchange of papers between the parties. A party may request an admission on either an issue of law or fact concerning all matters relevant, but not privileged, and within the knowledge of the opposing party. The responding party can remain silent, in which case the issue will be deemed admitted; specifically admit or deny each request; object on the ground some requests concern irrelevant or privileged matter; or refuse to answer, stating in detail why he cannot deny or admit as requested.

It is this last option that has posed the greatest difficulty for the courts. What are sufficient grounds for refusing to answer? Two problems surface immediately. First, when is some matter outside the knowledge of the party so that no answer can be made? The party clearly need not conduct a detailed search for information in order to answer, as that appears to place him in the position of proving the other side's case. Nonetheless, some inquiry must be made. Second, can a party refuse to answer on the ground that the issue concerned is the essential issue in dispute and to answer would be to concede the case? Under the federal rules, a party cannot object to an admission on the sole ground that it involves a core issue in the case. See Fed.Rule 36(a). Some state courts prohibit admissions on basic issues.

§ 3–27.   Objections to Information Sought

With the exception of requests for physical or mental examinations, discovery proceeds without court intervention unless some dispute arises. When a party objects to an inquiry made during the course of any of the discovery procedures described above, he may pursue one of two routes. The first is to answer all non-objectionable questions, registering an objection to those he refuses to answer. The party seeking discovery then can move for a court order compelling a response, at which time the examinee can explain the basis for his objections. The other alternative is for the examinee to move for a protective order to allow him to avoid responding. Under the first alternative the need for court intervention may never materialize, as the requesting party, after reviewing the responses that the party is willing to make, may decide that it is not necessary to pursue the unanswered questions.

If the court orders a response to be made and the requesting party continues to refuse, sanctions may be imposed, see § 3–28, infra. However, if the court upholds the objection, it may enter a wide range of protective orders, ranging from forbidding inquiry into certain matters, to allowing discovery but only under certain circumstances (e. g., a deposition placed under seal and allowed to be opened by court order). A good listing of the types of protective orders available to the court can be found in Fed.Rule 26(c).

The question of how to object to discovery raises another important problem—how to obtain immediate appellate review of court orders requiring or limiting discovery. In most judicial systems appeals are permissible only after a judgment on the merits has been reached. See §§ 7–1—7–5, infra. Interlocutory orders, such as discovery orders, must await the final judgment before being reviewed. In many cases this will mean that the order is never reviewed, as it will be most difficult to demonstate that the order, even if erroneous, was so prejudicial to the ultimate result as to merit a reversal. There are only two means available to the attorney to obtain immediate review under these circumstances. The first is to petition for the extraordinary writ of mandamus. See § 7–5, infra. Mandamus provides only very limited relief as it is restricted to situations in which some gross miscarriage of justice or abuse of discretion occurred in the trial court. For example, mandamus was granted to review an order requiring the defendants to submit to nine physical examinations; the challenge raised the constitutional rights of the defendants.

The second means of obtaining review is to refuse to obey the court order, be adjudged in contempt, and appeal from the final contempt judgment challenging the bases on which it was entered. This process is risky, however. No appeal
will be allowed if civil, rather than criminal, contempt is found. Further, if the appellate court
upholds the lower court's discovery order, the contempt penalty will remain in effect. Thus, in most
situations the trial court's discovery orders will be
final and binding.

§ 3–28. Sanctions

Every set of discovery rules contains a provision for sanctions in the event court intervention
is invoked, see, e. g., Fed.Rule 37. Most commonly, the court is permitted to assess expenses. A
party who forced an adjournment of a deposition,
or who fails to appear for a properly noticed deposition or to answer or respond to an otherwise
proper discovery request may be required to pay
any expenses incurred by the opponent because of
those tactics. In cases of wilful disobedience, the
court may dismiss the case or enter a default
judgment. Similarly, it may deem established all
matters about which the party refused to respond
or strike those matters from the pleadings. Finally, when the court has ordered a party to respond
to certain inquiries and he has refused to do so,
a contempt judgment may be entered, including a
possible jail sentence and fine.

3. SPECIFIC PROBLEMS

§ 3–29. Attorney Work-product

One of the serious problems that has faced courts having liberal discovery rules is how to prevent legal parasitism, by which one side in the litigation lessens its own investment and preparation by allowing the opponent to fully prepare the case and then discovering that attorney's work-product. To allow this kind of occurrence would destroy the adversary nature of the proceeding and debilitate the quality of the lawyering in the courts, as it would inhibit maximum trial preparation.

It generally is held that attorney-client privilege rules protect only direct communications between the attorney and the client, they do not protect information from witnesses, investigative reports, internal memorandums, etc. Thus, the United States Supreme Court developed the work-product rule for the federal courts. It totally exempts from discovery the mental impressions, conclusions, opinions or legal theories of the opposing attorney. Further, the attorney's other work product is not discoverable unless the person requesting access shows both need and that refusal to allow discovery would prejudice or cause extreme hardship to him. Hickman v. Taylor, 329 U.S. 495 (1947). The person requesting discovery must be able to show that there are no alternative means of obtaining the information and that it is vital to the preparation of the case. Several states have enacted the work-product rule as part of their discovery statutes, and the rule is now incorporated in the federal rules. See Fed.Rule 26 (b)(3).

Some problems have arisen in defining what is work-product. First, does it cover material gathered by persons other than the attorney, such as photographs or a surveillance report by an investigative agency? Second, is it limited to materials gathered solely in anticipation of trial or might it protect matter collected before it was reasonable to assume suit would be brought? The federal discovery rule attempts to answer these questions for the federal courts. It provides protection for all materials collected by the attorney *or his agent* and solely in anticipation of trial. These materials may be discovered only upon a showing of substantial need and undue hardship. Mental impressions remain totally protected. Witnesses and parties are permitted to obtain their own statements, made at an earlier time, without the required showing. This is in distinction to the state or common law work-product rule, which would protect this last category of data.

§ 3–30. Expert Witnesses

Discovery involving expert witnesses poses special problems. At the outset, they appear protected by the work-product rule in that it may be only through the ingenuity and hard work of the attorney that the expert witnesses were uncovered and their testimony developed for the case. Further, discovery of these witnesses may reveal in substantial part the theories and conclusions of the side retaining them. On the other hand, because of the complex or technical nature of most expert testimony, there is a definite need for the opposing side to have some idea of what to expect so as to be able to cross-examine adequately and introduce an effective rebuttal. Concerns about fair and effective trials appear to outweigh fears about parasitism in this context. .

In recognition of the special nature of this problem, the federal rules explicitly permit discovery of the name and of the substance of the testimony of any expert retained for use at trial. Fed.Rule 26(b)(4)(A). Discovery also is allowed of experts who are retained by counsel, but who will not testify at trial, if there are exceptional circumstances why the movant cannot obtain like evidence by other means. Fed.Rule 26(b)(4)(B). In this way one party cannot effectively control the case by retaining all the noted and available authorities in a field, using only those who support his client's case. To avoid a possible windfall to the requesting party who obtains discovery under this exception, the court is authorized to require that party to pay a portion of the fees and expenses related to the experts discovered.

The special expert rule does not cover all categories of experts. Experts who have an informal relationship with an attorney, acting merely as sources of information without being retained, fall within the general work-product rule. Similarly, in states not having a special expert rule, discovery will be governed by the work-product rule and permitted only when it would prejudice the requesting party to deny it. Finally, experts who also are employees of corporate parties and who were not hired for purposes of the particular piece of litigation at hand are fully discoverable as witnesses by either side.

§ 3–31. Insurance Agreements

In most states the fact of insurance is not admissible at trial and direct actions are not permitted against insurance companies. Injured parties must sue the insured and then seek reimbursement. These limitations are designed to protect the insurance industry from inflated verdicts entered by juries influenced by the deep pocket of the subrogor rather than the merits of the plaintiff's case. However, the injured party may obtain discovery of the defendant's insurance coverage. See Fed.Rule 26(b)(2). Discovery, though not relevant to the trial, is permitted in order to allow the party an opportunity to assess adequately the settlement value of the case. While this information may result in harder bargaining for larger settlements, it is felt that a fair settlement process requires full disclosure.

§ 3–32. Abuses and Proposals for Reform

The liberal, wide-open discovery rules used in most state and federal courts have accomplished much in the way of eliminating verdicts won primarily by surprise tactics. They also have been terribly abused. In particular, critics point to massive document discovery and countless, needless interrogatories. The constant overuse of these devices has resulted in raising substantially the cost of litigation. In many instances discovery has become a tool of delay and harassment. Enormous corporate parties can coerce settlements in suits by individuals by threatening them with long and involved discovery. Conversely, a corporation faced with enormous document demands or a ceaseless series of interrogatories may feel settlement is the only reasonable alternative. Whatever the cause, it is clear that justice is being subverted insofar as discovery is being used not to search out the truth, but to force settlement.

The ethics of these tactics should be seriously questioned. The attorneys are officers of the court as well as adversaries, and owe it the duty of seeking, not side-stepping, justice. Several judges, bar associations, and commentators have urged reforms to curb these abuses. Suggestions range from limiting the quantity of discovery to return-

ing to special pleading and simultaneously limiting
the scope of discovery. Increased court control
through pretrial conferences also has been suggested. At present, these reforms are in the em-
bryonic stage. However, it is clear that we can
expect some revisions and limitations on the discovery phase of litigation in the near future.

E.   PRETRIAL CONFERENCE

§ 3–33.   In General

Because of the increased liberalization of pleading requirements, the pretrial conference has become the point in time at which the case becomes
crystallized. The conference typically occurs after
discovery, when counsel, talking informally with
the judge, are able to agree as to what issues are in
dispute. They can plan the course of the trial
since they know what evidence and witnesses they
intend to introduce. In very complex litigation,
a series of conferences may be used to schedule
discovery and to structure the trial.

The judge has discretion to schedule a pretrial
conference in both state and federal systems, although some courts have provided by local rules
that conferences are mandatory in all cases. The
question whether pretrial conferences should be
mandatory or discretionary is tied to the perennial
debate on their ultimate usefulness. In simple
cases, is more time wasted in the conference, than

is saved at trial or is it really a means of coercing settlement? In complicated cases, are the trials actually simplified and better organized and therefore speedier or does the pretrial conference merely add another hurdle and more time to the case? There is no agreement on the answers to these questions. In a real sense it is the pretrial judge's instinctive belief (perhaps based on years of experience) regarding the utility of the conference that dictates its use in a given court.

§ 3–34. The Judge's Role

It is truly the judge who controls the effectiveness of the pretrial conference. The judge's interest, familiarity with the case, and belief as to the need to reach some agreement between the parties generally determines whether the parties actually will work toward some accord. The judge must tread a careful line between coercing the parties and helping them to reach reasonable conclusions. This problem has produced a difference of opinion as to whether the pretrial judge also should be assigned to try the case. If the pretrial and trial judges are different, then the expertise the judge gathered during the pretrial is lost at trial. Conversely, the incentive of the pretrial judge to totally familiarize himself with the case is lessened, which may result in a less effective pretrial. On the other hand, using different trial and pretrial judges lessens the coerciveness of suggestions made by the pretrial judge; the parties need not fear that a failure to agree to some concession proposed by the judge will be prejudicial at the trial. The pretrial judge functions more as an arbitrator or outside expert. At present, courts differ as to which way they resolve this dilemma.

Regardless of whether the pretrial conference and trial are before the same judge, there are certain questions regarding the proper exercise of the judge's power at the conference that continue to surface. The first is the propriety of the judge urging the parties to settle the case out of court. Courts and commentators are split on this issue. Most judges seem to feel that it is proper to suggest that a settlement may be appropriate once the actual issues are revealed, and that one of the purposes of the conference is to see if an agreement can be reached and trial avoided. However, it is improper to coerce the parties into the settlement. The problem is one of degree.

The second issue concerning the judge's power concerns whether he may force the parties to stipulate as to the issues. One of the purposes of the conference is to formulate the issues for trial, stipulating as to agreed-upon non-issues. However, if a party refuses to concede that something is a non-issue, should the court be able to force the stipulation? Most courts answer no; the court may require the parties to enter a formal stipulation only when they agree on specific issues.

The final question involving the pretrial judge's power concerns what sanctions may be applied if the parties fail to appear at the conference or refuse or fail to reveal certain information requested by the court, such as the witnesses who will be called or the evidence that will be introduced. It generally is recognized that the court may enter a default judgment or, in the case of a delinquent plaintiff, an involuntary dismissal with prejudice against parties whose counsel fail to appear at a scheduled conference. However, this sanction is so powerful that, as a practical matter, its use is strictly limited to situations in which the party has been exceptionally dilatory. This usually means that the counsel not only has failed to appear at the conference, but also generally has delayed the course of the litigation. A more common sanction is to limit the evidence to be used at the trial to only that which was revealed at the conference pursuant to the court's request. Typically, the issue arises in the context of a motion to amend the pretrial order and the court's "sanction" for the earlier failure is to deny that motion.

§ 3–35. Pretrial Orders

At the end of the pretrial conference, the judge enters a pretrial order incorporating all the parties' stipulations, the list of witnesses and evidence agreed upon, and any other matters that were decided at the conference. The order supersedes the pleadings and controls the remainder of the proceedings in that action. If the attorneys wish to introduce a new issue or additional evidence at trial, they must petition the court for relief. Relief will be allowed to prevent manifest injustice, but it is within the discretion of the court to require adherence to the original order. Thus, the trial judge will weigh carefully the possible prejudice to the opposing party (who may have relied on the order when preparing for trial), the importance of the proposed change, and whether the movant was dilatory in not introducing the proposed matter at the conference. If the movant succeeds, the relief typically will take the form of an amendment to the pretrial order.

IV. ADJUDICATION WITHOUT TRIAL

A. SUMMARY JUDGMENT

§ 4–1. In General

Summary judgment is a procedure by which a party can obtain a final binding determination on the merits without the necessity of a full trial. It differs from trial motions, such as the directed verdict, which also result in a final binding judgment, primarily because it is made earlier. A motion for summary judgment is distinguished from other pretrial motions to dismiss, demurrers or judgments on the pleadings because outside evidence is produced and the court is not limited to the pleadings in making its decision. Indeed, it is common for the rules governing demurrers or motions for failure to state a claim for relief to provide that, if the movant introduces outside matter, the motion automatically is converted into one for summary judgment. A wide variety of outside material may be used, including affidavits, depositions, admissions and even interrogatories. The key in deciding whether the material is properly before the court is whether it would be admissible under the rules of evidence at trial.

While the main purpose of summary judgment is to avoid unnecessary trials, it also can function to simplify the trial. Most judicial systems provide for some form of partial or interlocutory summary judgment by which only liability may be determined summarily or certain issues may be eliminated from the case on summary judgment. See, e. g., Fed.Rules 56(c), (d). In addition, a party may move for summary judgment in order to force his opponent to reveal some of his case in resisting the motion.

Although summary judgment obviates the need for a trial, it does not impinge upon any jury trial rights. This is because the standard for obtaining summary judgment requires in part a finding that there is no fact issue to send to the jury, see § 4–2, infra. The court does not weigh the evidence and decide that one party would necessarily succeed if the case went to a jury. Rather, it determines that there are no factual questions for the jury to decide.

§ 4–2. Grounds for Obtaining

The grounds for obtaining a summary judgment are threefold: there must be no *genuine issue* of *material* fact and the movant must be entitled to a judgment *as a matter of law*. See Fed.Rule 56(c). A party cannot resist a summary judgment motion simply by suggesting she is in disagreement with the movant's statement of facts. There must be a genuine or real dispute over certain factual issues. This typically requires the opposing party to introduce contradictory evidence, not merely conflicting allegations. Further, the facts in dispute must be central or material to the case. Disputes over irrelevant or minor facts will not bar summary judgment as, by definition, they will not affect the outcome even if a trial is had. Finally, the law governing the case must mandate a judgment for the movant. If any one of these three criteria is not met, the motion will be denied and the case sent to trial.

§ 4–3. Burden of Proof

A very important factor on summary judgment motions is the placement of the burden of proof. The movant necessarily has the initial burden of showing that the summary judgment standard has been met. She can, and typically does, introduce outside evidence to meet this burden. In general, that evidence is viewed in the light most favorable to the opposing party. Even with that rule of interpretation, the movant often may have shown sufficient grounds for obtaining summary judgment.

An important question arises as to what burdens are placed on the non-movant to resist the motion. In some state systems it is permissible for the opposing party merely to rest on the well-pleaded allegations in his pleadings, noting the conflict between them and the movant's evidence. See, e. g., Cal.Civ.Proc.Code § 437c. This approach places a very minimal burden on the nonmovant and, as a practical matter, means that summary judgment is almost impossible to obtain, except when the movant is resting her motion on the presence of an affirmative defense not rebutted by the pleadings.   In the federal courts, and in several state courts, the opposing party is not permitted to survive summary judgment on the basis of his pleadings, alone, unless the movant did not meet her initial burden.   If the movant's papers show that no genuine issue of material fact exists, then the burden shifts to the opposing party to introduce outside evidence rebutting this conclusion, see Fed.Rule 56(e).   If he fails to introduce any outside evidence then the movant's evidence will be taken as true and in most cases this will result in summary judgment being granted. This approach of shifting the burden of proof to the opposing party was adopted so that summary judgment could act to pierce the pleadings and allow the court to assess the proof.   To ameliorate some of the burden on the non-movant, another provision authorizes him to meet his burden by showing why he is unable at that time to present evidence in opposition, see Fed.Rule 56(f).   If the court finds these reasons to be valid, it may deny or postpone summary judgment.

§ 4–4.   Credibility as a Fact Issue

One of the most difficult problems on a motion for summary judgment is when to allow a party to overcome an otherwise properly supported summary judgment motion on the ground that material facts will have to be proven by the testimony of witnesses, whose credibility can be determined only by a jury. To the extent that this argument is accepted without reservation, summary judgment is almost impossible to obtain if any of the key evidence introduced on the motion consists of depositions or affidavits of witnesses or parties.

The decision to deny summary judgment when a credibility issue is raised varies from system to system and even from judge to judge, depending, at least in part, on the level of their concern that the procedure not be allowed to impinge on jury trial rights. In some states a specific provision exists in the summary judgment rule granting the court discretion to deny summary judgment whenever "the only proof of a material fact offered in support of the summary judgment is an affidavit or declaration made by an individual who was the sole witness to such fact." Cal.Civ.Proc.Code § 437c. This type of provision tips the balance in favor of a full trial. There is no comparable provision in the federal rules and the federal courts generally have held that an unsupported allegation that credibility is in issue will not suffice to overcome summary judgment. The party must introduce facts showing why a witness' credibility is in question. This typically requires evidence that the witness is not disinterested (i. e., he is a party) or that the determination of an issue of fact rests on the state of mind or motive of the actor so that it ultimately must turn on that person's credibility as to what was in his mind at a given time. However, the court will not weigh or assess the actual credibility of any witness— that is the jury's role. Rather, it will decide if there is reason to believe that credibility may be determinative.

§ 4–5. Procedure

Although the exact timing of summary judgment motions varies in each judicial system, a few general observations about the procedure on these motions can be made. Any party may move for summary judgment; cross-motions are possible. In that event, the court decides each motion separately. The fact that both parties moved does not establish that there is no genuine issue of material fact. Further, a court may order summary judgment for the opposing party, if it finds that as a matter of law judgment should be in his favor. However, the court generally cannot enter a summary judgment without a motion by at least one of the parties before it.

Typically, there will be a summary judgment hearing, although this may not be required and the court may decide the motion on the basis of the papers, alone. If there is a hearing, the parties will be allowed to engage in oral argument supporting their positions.

B. DEFAULT JUDGMENT

§ 4-6. Types of Default

There are essentially three types of default. In the first, the defendant never appears or answers in response to the plaintiff's complaint. In the second the defendant makes an appearance, but fails to file a formal answer or appear at trial. Both of these situations are specifically dealt with in specially designed rules present in each court system. In the third, the defendant fails to comply with some court order during the pretrial proceedings and the court enters a default judgment as a penalty. Authority for penalty defaults may be found in most discovery rules and they have been recognized as within the inherent equitable power of the court in order to force compliance or cooperation at the pretrial conference stage.

The denomination of a particular case as falling into one of these three default situations has important consequences on the procedure that is utilized for obtaining the judgment, see § 4-7, infra, and the party's ability to set aside the judgment, see § 6-1, infra. However, all three situations have the same impact on the defendant, insofar as they all treat his default as a concession on liability. The immediate effect of a ruling that a default is involved is to find for plaintiff on the merits.

§ 4–7. Procedure

When the defendant defaults at the outset and the plaintiff moves to declare him in default, one of two procedures applies. If a sum certain (i. e., liquidated damages) is being sought, the clerk may enter a default. If not, the judge must enter the default and hold a hearing at which plaintiff will be required to prove the amount of damages, not liability. The plaintiff's ad damnum sets the ceiling on damages, but does not guarantee that that amount will be recovered. The defendant may appear at the damages hearing and may demand a jury trial on that issue. This right is largely chimerical as the defendant is not given any formal notice of the damages hearing and thus typically will not appear.

When the defendant has made an appearance and then defaulted, only the court may enter a default judgment and notice must be sent to the defendant prior to the damages hearing. Further, defendant has the right to have all the subsequent papers in the action served on him. A failure to send the prescribed notice is an automatic ground for setting aside the judgment. The damages hearing proceeds just as in the case of a default by non-appearance. The rationale for including a mandatory notice requirement in this situation is that the defendant has shown some interest in the litigation by making the initial appearance. Thus, there is some concern that the later default occurred as a result of the lawyer's failure to comply with various procedural provisions, rather than as a result of the conscious decision of the party. The notice provides some protection against this occurrence and further assures the defaulting party the opportunity of making a timely appeal.

The defendant may be found to have appeared and defended, not defaulted. In that event special notice need not be sent for the damages hearing. Further, a motion to reopen the judgment and have a trial on the merits often will be viewed less favorably than in the case of a default because the court already has had an opportunity to explore the issues in an adversarial context. See generally § 6–1, infra. Thus, it is important to determine what constitutes an appearance sufficient to invoke the default judgment rule's protections, but not so active as to be deemed a full defense. In general, if the defendant files any pretrial motions short of an answer, or even more informally informs the court and opposing party of his intention to make an appearance, the court will treat the case as one in which the defendant has appeared and then defaulted. More difficult is the problem of how to treat the case when defendant has filed a responsive pleading, but then failed to appear. On the one hand, he has placed the case in issue, not conceding liability and the court should require the plaintiff to prove liability as well as damages before rendering judgment. On the other hand, since the defendant is not present at trial, there is not a truly adversarial proceeding and perhaps the court should treat it as a default with liability conceded and a hearing on damages after notice has been sent to the defendant. Not surprisingly, the courts are split on this issue. If calling the defendant's failure to be present at trial a default will provide grounds for reopening the judgment, the answer frequently will be deemed an appearance and the defendant's subsequent conduct a default.

The penalty default situation has posed special procedural concerns for the courts. Some courts have treated it as a default after appearance. Others have ruled it outside those protections. Most important is not the notice, since the court in ordering the penalty to be imposed typically notifies the parties. Rather, the issue is whether the court can rule that the defendant has conceded the entire case—liability and damages— and whether the court can award the plaintiff in excess of the ad damnum as a penalty. If the situation is treated as falling within the general default provisions, the answer to both of these questions is no. The courts are split on this question and the Supreme Court to date has not ruled on it.

C. VOLUNTARY AND INVOLUNTARY DISMISSAL

§ 4–8. Voluntary Dismissals

All judicial systems provide some means by which a plaintiff may voluntarily dismiss the case without court approval. This may occur when upon further investigation the plaintiff determines that she really does not have a claim worth pursuing or when the parties have settled the suit out of court. Countervailing considerations suggest that some limitations be placed on this procedure. People should be encouraged to file suit only when they are serious about pursuing it to judgment. Unrestricted voluntary dismissals would allow plaintiffs to harass defendants and present serious potential for abuse. Thus, the federal rules provide the plaintiff only one automatic right to a voluntary dismissal without prejudice, see Fed.Rule 41(a). If the same suit is filed again and another voluntary dismissal is sought and granted, it will be entered with prejudice, thereby preventing the action from being filed a third time. The plaintiff can voluntarily dismiss an action after the defendant has answered only with the consent of the defendant or by obtaining court approval. Similar restrictions exist in most state provisions.

§ 4–9. Involuntary Dismissals: Failure to Prosecute

A court can enter an involuntary dismissal for failure to prosecute. The defendant typically moves for this dismissal on the ground that plaintiff has failed to take appropriate steps to move the case to trial, has failed to appear at scheduled hearings or conferences, or continually has delayed or sought continuances to lengthen normal time periods. If the court grants the motion, the case will be dismissed with prejudice on the merits, unless the court specifically stipulates otherwise—a very rare occurrence. Thus, involuntary dismissals are granted sparingly and usually only when the plaintiff has been particularly dilatory.

Some provisions, such as Federal Rule 41(b), leave the decision to enter an involuntary dismissal totally within the discretion of the trial court. Others, such as the California Code, give some further direction to the court, permitting a dismissal only two years after the filing of the complaint and mandating dismissal when five years of inactivity or dilatoriness is shown. Within that period, however, the court can exercise its discretion to determine if the plaintiff's lack of action amounts to a total failure to prosecute. Cal.Civ.Proc.Code § 583.

V. THE TRIAL

A. THE PROCESS

§ 5-1. A General Description

Once a case has proceeded through discovery and survived any pretrial motions that may have been made, it will be placed on the trial docket of the court and a date for trial assigned. At that time, if no continuances or postponements have occurred, the parties and their counsel must appear before the judge to begin the trial.

Both jury and non-jury trials follow the same general rules of order, although the outset of the trial differs in a jury case as time must be spent choosing a jury to sit in the case. The order of presentation may vary slightly from court to court, but the general rules are as follows. Plaintiff's counsel followed by defendant's attorney each make opening statements, explaining what they intend to prove. The plaintiff's witnesses and evidence are examined and cross-examined. Then the defendant's witnesses and evidence are introduced, with similar rights of examination and cross-examination. The plaintiff and defendant then may be allowed to introduce rebuttal evidence. After all the evidence has been submitted, each side makes closing arguments summarizing the evidence supporting their respective positions. Plaintiff again typically summarizes first, but has

[*149*]

a right of rebuttal after the defendant's closing remarks have been made. If there is no jury, the judge then will evaluate the evidence and render a judgment. If a jury is involved, the judge instructs the jurors as to the law to be applied. In a few states the judge may comment on the evidence. However, in most jurisdictions this would be improper and the judge is authorized only to give an impartial summary of the evidence. The jury then renders a verdict and the judge enters a judgment on it.

§ 5–2. Rules of Evidence

The trial process is governed by rules of evidence. Each court system has its own set of evidentiary rules and the character of the proceeding may vary somewhat depending on what types of evidence are permitted to be introduced. Most generally, proper evidence or testimony is that which is relevant and not privileged or hearsay. Definitions of relevance, privilege, and hearsay fill the law books and are more fully explored in the separate course on evidence. For our purposes a brief description will suffice.

The relevance of specific evidence is determined in relation to the scope of the issues in the case at hand. Irrelevant evidence is excluded in order to aid the trier of fact in focusing on what actually is in issue. Privileged matter is excluded to protect the privacy of individuals in certain relationships (i. e. doctor-patient, lawyer-client). Persons in a privileged relationship need not reveal any communications that occurred between them. The law places a greater value on preserving the sanctity of those relationships than on the need to find truth based on all the possible evidence. Hearsay is defined as an out of court statement offered to prove the fact or truth of the matter stated. The rules defining hearsay are riddled with exceptions. In general, they are designed to prevent the use of evidence that is thought to be unreliable. Hearsay is deemed inherently unreliable because there is no opportunity to cross-examine the actual person who made the statement.

Counsel must raise evidentiary objections immediately or they will be waived. In addition, in the case of privileged information, the parties to the relationship can waive their right to claim privilege by their conduct. If an objection is sustained, the evidence will be stricken or the jury will be instructed not to take it into account in rendering the verdict. A judge trial often is a little less rigid in adhering strictly to the evidentiary rules, as it is assumed that the judge will disregard improper evidence and consider only proper evidence. Thus, there is less need to object as frequently. Similarly, there is less fear that improper evidence will be considered, if the court sustains an objection. In the jury setting, there is a serious question whether it is reasonable to expect the jury to disregard improper evidence that is mentioned in its presence, even if instructed to do so, or whether the jury has been so prejudiced that a mistrial should be called.

B. JURY TRIAL

1. IN GENERAL

§ 5–3. The Jury—Its History, Character and Function

Jury trial is a fundamental part of the Anglo-American dispute resolution process. It was first formalized in the Twelfth Century in England during the reign of King Henry II and it fast became the hallmark of the common law courts. The historic jury was composed of twelve men from the community. These men were asked to determine what were the actual facts underlying a controversy and the judge then would apply the law. The jury's decision had to be unanimous. While the form of the jury remained the same when it was transplanted to the American colonies, it also assumed additional symbolic meanings. Jury trial became a symbol of American freedom or popular justice versus the king's justice. Although the need to establish our independence has long since passed, jury trial remains at the core of the civil court system.

In recent years several state and federal courts have modified the original character of the jury so that juries have been composed of less than twelve members and non-unanimous verdicts have been permitted. These changes have been in an effort to reduce the costliness of jury trials. Smaller juries should be selected more rapidly, and their deliberations should be shorter simply because there are fewer individual opinions to consider. Non-unanimous verdicts lessen the possibility of a deadlock, with its attendant need for a new trial. The United States Supreme Court has approved the use of six member juries in civil cases, Colgrove v. Battin, 413 U.S. 149 (1973), and non-unanimous verdicts in criminal cases, Apodaca v. Oregon, 400 U.S. 901 (1970). It has not yet ruled on non-unanimous civil verdicts, but its reasoning in the criminal field suggests that they may be upheld in the future. The Court ruled that the character of the jury trial was not part of the historic or constitutional right and that, based on the studies to date, it could find no proof of a qualitative difference between verdicts rendered under either system. Thus, the lower courts are left to decide for themselves whether to modify the twelve person, unanimous jury, and the character of the jury may vary depending on the court in which you are proceeding.

The role of the jury remains unchanged, however. The jury is to decide questions of fact; the judge determines issues of law. This distribution of responsibility recognizes the special qualities of the jury and the judge. The jury is present to conform legal standards to current experience. For example, if a case involves the interpretation of a contract, a question of fact is presented and a jury decision on the meaning of certain contract language relies on community experience as to common practices when persons enter into a contract. The judge's role is to provide rules to bind litigants in the future so that the community can know how to conduct future dealings. Thus, in contract disputes the judge decides whether a legally binding or valid contract has been made. The jury decides all issues of credibility as those are questions of fact. The judge also determines if the law allows relief under the facts as determined by the jury.

This line between issues of fact and of law is not always easy to ascertain and the case reports are filled with cases in which judges improperly have removed issues from the jury. The appropriate delineation of the jury's role is further clouded because of the jury nullification process. Most often, the judge instructs the jury on the law applicable to a given set of facts and the jury not only determines the facts, but also applies the law to those facts. In areas where the law has been slow to develop, the jury may decide to dispense justice, ignoring the law. Illustratively, there are negligence cases in which it is quite clear that the jury ignored rules of contributory negligence that would bar plaintiff's recovery and simply took the plaintiff's negligence into account in assessing the damages—establishing a comparative negligence standard before it was adopted by the courts. Jury proponents argue that this is one of the special functions of the jury and is simply a means of modernizing the law in light of current community mores. However, allowing the jury to tamper with the law presents potential dangers in situations, such as in the civil rights field, in which local community standards are inconsistent with more general, indeed constitutional, national standards.

2. SCOPE OF JURY TRIAL RIGHTS

§ 5-4. Sources of Jury Trial Rights

The authority for demanding a jury trial in a civil action may derive from one of three sources. The first, and broadest, is constitutional. Federal and state constitutions set the minimal standards for jury trial in their respective judicial systems. The legislature has the power to authorize jury trial in cases not within the constitutional guarantee. Thus, the second jury trial source is statutory and represents those situations in which the legislature in establishing a particular cause of action has granted a right to a jury trial. Finally, the trial court always has the equitable power to impanel a jury, although in those instances the jury will be advisory only and the judge may accept or disregard its findings.

The major problems in determining the scope of jury trial rights have been in the constitutional area. It should be noted that the federal constitutional jury provision (Seventh Amendment) is not binding on the states so that they have been free to develop their own scheme of civil jury trial rights for their courts. All but four of the states (Colorado, Utah, Louisiana, and Wyoming) have constitutional provisions similar to the federal and in those four states statutory jury trial rights exist. Further, with the exception of four other states (Georgia, North Carolina, Tennessee, and Texas), which provide a jury trial in equity, all the states appear to interpret their constitutional and statutory provisions similarly to the federal courts. Thus, the following discussion will explore civil jury trial rights in the federal courts as that provides the best model for study.

§ 5–5. Constitutional Juries in Non-statutory Actions

The Seventh Amendment to the United States Constitution provides for a right to jury trial "in suits at common law" exceeding twenty dol-

lars. Thus, the test for determining whether the
Seventh Amendment is properly invoked requires
an inquiry into history and whether the action
was one that could have been brought at common
law, rather than in an equity court. This inquiry
can be most complex since separate equity and
law courts no longer exist; the federal courts
now are empowered to try all claims. Further,
the availability of joinder of claims and parties
under modern rules of procedure presents situations unknown at common law.

In essence, the Supreme Court has developed
the following test. The right to a jury trial depends on the nature of the *issue* on which a jury
trial is demanded. If the underlying nature of the
issue is legal, then it matters not that the type of
proceeding involved (i. e., class or derivative suits
or interpleader proceedings) historically was
available only in equity. A jury trial is required
on that issue. Ross v. Bernhard, 396 U.S. 531
(1970). Further, it does not matter whether
the legal issue is introduced by way of the plaintiff's claim or by the defendant's answer, it requires a jury trial. In cases in which there is a
common legal issue to both a legal and an equitable claim, that issue must be tried first by the
jury, before the judge can rule on the equitable
claim. Beacon Theatres, Inc. v. Westover, 359
U.S. 500 (1959).

Focusing on the issue rather than the action as a whole and ordering the trial to permit a jury trial on any common legal issues represents a definite departure from history. Traditionally, the equity clean-up doctrine governed and in suits first properly lodged in equity, the judge would determine any incidental legal issues. The Supreme Court has specifically rejected the clean-up doctrine, exhibiting a definite preference for jury trial. Not all the states have followed this approach. The basis for this movement away from the rigid historical test is the Court's belief that the availability of new legal remedies necessarily reduces the scope of equity, which was developed to apply only when there were no adequate legal remedies. Under the current standard, history alone does not reveal whether an action will be deemed a "suit at common law" for Seventh Amendment purposes. Rather, the court will determine whether circumstances now merit the characterization of a type of claim or issue as legal and within the scope of the constitutional jury trial guarantee.

This same flexible approach appears in the current standard for determining the legal nature of an issue. The historical treatment of an issue still is important. For example, fraud remains equitable and no jury trial right attaches. Further, the remedy being sought aids in deciding whether a jury is required so that suits seeking

only injunctive relief, being traditionally equitable, should not require a jury. However, the
form of relief is not always determinative and,
once again, if new applicable legal remedies exist,
the claim may be treated as legal. For example,
a claim for an accounting was deemed legal for
jury trial purposes since the availability of mas-
ters to assist the jury removed the traditional reason for referring those claims to equity and the
judge. Dairy Queen, Inc. v. Wood, 369 U.S. 469
(1962). Further, the Supreme Court has suggested that a proper consideration in deciding whether a jury trial should be used may be the "practical abilities and limitations of juries." Ross v.
Bernhard, 396 U.S. 531, 538 n. 10 (1970). To date
the Court has not explained how this last factor
may be utilized.

§ 5–6. Constitutional Juries in Statutory Actions

In most cases the fact that an action is statutory does not aid in determining whether the
Seventh Amendment applies. If the Congress
specifically provides for jury trial, then the constitutional question need not be reached. In the
absence of a statutory jury trial right, the right
to a jury trial will depend on whether the issues
involved are legal or equitable in nature. Since
the majority of liability statutes merely codify
pre-existing common law rights, most statutory
actions involve the same analytical jury trial

problems as non-statutory actions, see § 5–5, supra.

An important issue peculiar to statutory actions does arise, however. That is whether the
Congress can effectively declare something equitable and outside the scope of the Seventh Amendment, even though historically the issue would
have been given a jury trial in a suit at common
law. It appears that if the statute involved provides for a statutory proceeding before an administrative board or a specialized court, rather
than an action in a general district court, and if
there is evidence supporting the need for non-
jury treatment, the enactment will withstand constitutional attack. See Katchen v. Landy, 382 U.
S. 323 (1966) (bankruptcy court), and NLRB v.
Jones & Laughlin Steel Corp., 301 U.S. 1 (1937),
(administrative tribunal). The answer is not so
clear when the statute in question provides for
trial in the general federal district courts. The
Supreme Court has upheld the constitutional right
to a jury trial in statutory actions in the regular
courts when the actions had common law analogs
and the only arguments for non-jury trial were
unsupported allegations that the jury would not
function so as to do justice and was inconsistent
with the policies underlying the enactments. See
Curtis v. Loether, 415 U.S. 189 (1974), (claim
jury prejudice would undermine enforcement of
civil rights act), and Pernell v. Southall Realty,

416 U.S. 363 (1974) (claim Congressional intent to provide speedy remedy in landlord-tenant area inconsistent with use of jury trial). The Court has not yet ruled on the question whether clearly expressed Congressional intent to create a statutory cause of action to be enforced in the courts without the availability of a jury trial is sufficient to place the action outside the scope of the Seventh Amendment.

§ 5-7. Demand Requirements

In a few state courts, jury trial is used unless a non-jury trial is requested. In most states and in the federal system the converse is true. Unless a jury trial is demanded within the statutory period, the right to trial by jury is waived. Although the court has the discretion to allow an untimely demand, that discretion is exercised sparingly and in most instances there is no relief from waiver.

Demand requirements have withstood constitutional challenge. They are not viewed as terribly burdensome to the parties and thus their impact on constitutional jury rights is minimal. Further, that minimal effect is deemed justifiable because of the generally recognized need for the courts to be able to exercise some docket control. The ability to determine at an early stage whether an action requires a jury permits the courts to schedule their cases accordingly and in that way better administer their caseloads. Thus, the attorney always should check the specific demand requirements of the court in which suit is brought in order not to fail inadvertently to make a timely request.

3. MEANS OF CONTROLLING THE JURY

§ 5–8. In General

There are various methods or procedures designed to ensure that the jury performs its proper role. The evidentiary rules, for example, limit the jury to considering only legally relevant and generally reliable evidence in determining the facts. When the judge sustains objections to proposed evidence or testimony, he protects the jury from considering possibly irrelevant and prejudicial matters. Similarly, the judge's instructions to the jury describe and define the proper scope of its inquiry, prescribing who has the burden of persuasion on the facts in issue. Of course, the effectiveness of this control depends totally on whether the jury follows the judge's charges. Finally, the attorneys may poll the jury after the verdict has been announced to make certain that each of the jurors is in agreement with and understands the judgment. The following sections will describe some other means of jury control.

§ 5-9. Selection Process

Even though the actual jury selection process
varies from court to court, a few generalized
statements can be made. The process begins by
notices sent to community members by the court
clerk requesting them to appear and be placed in
the jury pool (called the *array*). Some potential
jurors may exclude themselves if they fit under
statutory exceptions. Excuses from jury service
usually are limited to vocational categories (i. e.
firemen or doctors), to health reasons or to in-
competence (i. e. cannot speak English). Jurors
also may be excused if they can show that it would
be an undue hardship for them to have to serve.
Whatever process of selection is used at this stage
must be designed to obtain a broad cross-section
of the community. No group can be systematically excluded or the attorney may successfully
challenge the array on constitutional grounds.

Individual jurors from the array are selected to
sit on a specific case (*panel*) after being examined
before the court. That screening is called *voir
dire*. In some courts the judge asks the jurors
all questions and the attorneys submit in advance
any questions they would like answered. In other
courts the attorneys themselves conduct voir
dire. The purpose in either situation is to determine if any of the prospective jurors is likely to
be so biased or prejudiced in the case that he or

she could not reach an independent judgment based on the facts presented. If so, the attorney may *challenge for cause* and, if the judge agrees, that person will be disqualified. If the judge permits the juror to remain, the same challenge can be raised on appeal from the final judgment and the verdict overturned if the trial court's decision was an abuse of discretion. Attorneys also are given a limited number of *peremptory challenges* by which they can reject a potential juror without stating the reason. This device allows the attorney to try to select those persons he feels are most likely to be sympathetic to his client or to the type of evidence that will be presented. Further, he can reject persons who do not reveal enough bias to merit a challenge for cause, but he feels will be prejudiced against his client or case. In this way the attorneys shape the character of each jury.

§ 5–10.　Types of Verdicts

The type of verdict used may help to assure that the jury performs only its assigned function of resolving issues of fact. Most frequently a *general verdict* is requested. The judge instructs the jury on the law and the jury applies the law to the facts as it finds them, reporting to the court only which party wins and the relief, if any, to be awarded. Obviously, the general verdict provides little jury control as there is no way to determine on what the verdict is based. Further, in the event of an appeal, the reviewing court must reverse if there has been an error involving any of the alternative claims, theories or defenses presented to the jury since it is not certain whether the jury rested its decision on findings supported by improper evidence or on other grounds.

The *special verdict* is at the opposite end of the spectrum. The court requests the jury to make specific findings of fact and the judge applies the law to those facts and renders judgment accordingly. The special verdict is designed to make the trial process more scientific and prevents the jury from acting on bias or ignoring the law. In this way, the number of appellate reversals should be reduced. The device has been criticized, however, as it makes the jury deliberation process much more difficult and slow. Additionally, the exercise of such tight control over the jury is challenged as inconsistent with the historic power of the jury to bring the community's standards to bear on a case, even when those mores differ from specific laws. Despite these objections, any party may request the court to utilize a special verdict or the court may decide on its own to do so. It is totally within the discretion of the trial judge to decide whether a special verdict may be utilized.

As a middle ground between special and general verdicts, the court may utilize a *general ver-*

dict with interrogatories. The judge instructs the jury on the law and requests a general verdict as described above. Additionally, however, certain specific cross-check questions are submitted that will enable the court to see whether the verdict rendered is consistent with the facts as found. The judge is not supposed to try to restrict the jury by including so many detailed questions that the jury has no discretion regarding the size or type of award rendered. Rather, the questions typically are designed to make certain that the liability determination is consistent with the facts —that the law was applied properly. Specific rules usually outline the options for a judge when the answers to the interrogatories do not support the verdict. If the answers are internally consistent, but simply cannot be reconciled with the verdict, Fed. Rule 49(b) authorizes the judge to return the case to the jury for further consideration, to enter a verdict consistent with the specific answers, or to set the case for a new trial. If some of the answers are not consistent internally, as well as contrary to the verdict, then the judge's options are to return the case to the jury or order a new trial.

§ 5–11. Impeachment of the Verdict

Although a verdict may appear proper on its face, a variety of circumstances may have occurred that would show that the jury did not function properly and the judgment should be set aside. For example, the jurors may have considered evidence not introduced at the trial and thus not subject to examination and cross-examination. They may have visited the scene of the accident on their own or one of the jurors may have "testified" to the others on the matters in question. A juror may have failed to reveal during voir dire his or her relationship with one of the parties or their attorneys. The jury may not have reached a unanimous verdict on liability and damages, but instead may have used a quotient verdict with each member simply writing down the judgment felt to be fair and then dividing the sum total by the number of jury members. In any one of these or a number of other circumstances, the parties have been deprived of their right to a totally impartial, properly functioning jury, which considers only court controlled evidence and reaches a unanimous decision on the basis of that evidence alone.

A problem that exists in any of the above situations is what evidence may be introduced to prove jury misconduct to the possible prejudice of the losing party. The sanctity and total privacy of jury deliberations has been seen as the best means of assuring a fair trial because it encourages the jurors to feel free to discuss and vote their conscience since they know that all that takes place will not be revealed publicly. Thus, any evidence of juror misconduct that requires an inquiry into the deliberation process is suspect. Further, it is argued that there is no way to assure a completely impartial jury as each member necessarily brings to the trial certain individual feelings or predispositions; all that we should be trying to obtain is a cross-section of the community so that various prejudices will be counterbalanced. Finally, the cost of overturning the verdict because the jury did not act properly is to require an entire new trial with no assurance of reaching a more just result.

Given these arguments, it should not be surprising that the historic and most widely followed rule (the Mansfield rule) has been that juror affidavits cannot be used to impeach the verdict. However, the verdict may be impeached on the basis of evidence from other sources. For example, if a person observed the jury visiting the scene of the accident, he could testify to that effect. Many courts that follow the Mansfield rule also permit testimony that reveals perjury during voir dire as that does not necessitate an intrusion into the deliberation process itself, but challenges earlier happenings. A minority of courts follow the Iowa rule, which allows the verdict to be challenged on the basis of juror testimony concerning overt acts of other jury members that may have been prejudicial. The impeaching evidence cannot rest on the state of mind or feelings of individual jury members, however. Thus, under the Iowa rule, a verdict could be impeached on the basis of a juror affidavit to the effect that one of the members told the jury that she had a family emergency and urged them to reach a quick decision and terminate their discussion so that she could return home. An affidavit stating that one of the jurors had received news of a family emergency and had acted under great stress and hastily when reaching the verdict will not be allowed. Under the Mansfield rule, neither affidavit is permissible. The federal courts have adopted a compromise position on this question. Federal Rule of Evidence 606 allows the introduction of juror testimony only to show that prejudicial outside evidence was brought into the jury room or extraneous influences were improperly brought to bear on any juror.

C. TRIAL AND POST–TRIAL MOTIONS

1. DIRECTED VERDICT

§ 5–12. Principles Governing

Directed verdict motions may be made by either party at the close of their opponent's evidence. The theory behind the motion is that there is insufficient evidence to go to the jury or that the evidence is so compelling that only one result could follow, so that to save trial time the court should enter a judgment for the movant. Although the effect of a successful directed verdict motion is to take the case away from the jury, the Supreme Court has ruled that directed verdict motions do not violate the constitutional jury trial guarantee since comparable procedures—i. e., demurrers to the evidence—existed at common law. Galloway v. United States, 319 U.S. 372 (1943).

The issue before the trial court on a directed verdict motion is whether there is sufficient evidence to raise a fact issue. In order to answer this question, the court will view the evidence in the light most favorable to the nonmovant. In some jurisdictions this means that the judge will not consider the moving party's evidence. More commonly, the court will review all the evidence, allowing conflicting evidence to cancel out and deciding any credibility problems in favor of the nonmovant.

There are two different formulations of the standard for granting a directed verdict: the scintilla test and the substantial evidence test. Under the scintilla test the court will deny the motion and refer the case to the jury if there is a scintilla, or *any*, evidence on which the jury might possibly render a verdict for the nonmovant. Under the substantial evidence test, the court will grant the motion unless there is sufficient or substantial evidence suggesting that the jury might decide for the nonmovant. The difference between these two tests reflects the different attitudes that courts have with regard to the importance of jury trial and the amount of control that properly may be exercised by the judge over the jury. The modern trend has been toward the use of the substantial evidence test.

2. JUDGMENT NOTWITHSTANDING THE VERDICT

§ 5–13. Principles Governing

The major difference between a motion for judgment notwithstanding the verdict (JNOV) and a directed verdict motion is the timing. A JNOV motion is made to the trial judge after the verdict is rendered (usually within 10 days of the verdict) and seeks a judgment contrary to it on the ground that there was insufficient evidence for the jury to find as it did. Its primary use is when there is some overriding issue of law that would indicate that the jury verdict is erroneous. The court deciding a JNOV motion does not weigh the evidence any more than it does on a directed verdict motion. Rather, it considers whether there was any evidence supporting the jury's verdict in light of the law governing the case.

The JNOV motion serves several important functions. At the outset its availability encourages the judge to ease back on the directed ver-

[*171*]

dict motion. At the time of that earlier motion the judge may not be ready to decide whether the evidence is sufficient to warrant a judgment. The judge can submit the case to the jury, and in many cases the verdict should be the same as would have occurred on the directed verdict motion. When the judge's inclination and the jury's disposition agree, quarrels (and appeals) about directed verdicts cannot arise. When they disagree, the court still can impose its will. Additional time savings occur in the event of an appeal. If a JNOV is reversed, the jury's verdict is entered. If a directed verdict is reversed, a new trial is necessary so that the case can be sent to the jury. This ultimate savings in trial time on JNOV may be offset, however, by the fact that more appeals may be taken from JNOV rulings than from directed verdicts, because the difference between the judge and jury is only speculative in the directed verdict context.

In the federal courts, a directed verdict motion is a prerequisite to a JNOV motion. See Fed. Rule 50(b). This is because there is no historic common law analog for the JNOV. JNOV motions have withstood the challenge that they violate constitutional jury trial rights solely on the ground that they are delayed directed verdict motions and directed verdicts were authorized in common law actions. Since the states are not bound by the Seventh Amendment, they are free to treat these two motions differently and several states allow JNOV motions to be made even though no directed verdict motion was interposed.

3. NEW TRIAL

§ 5–14. Principles Governing

Judicial systems typically provide some means by which a party dissatisfied with the first proceeding may request a new trial. In this way, the trial judge is given an opportunity to correct any errors that may have occurred during the first trial. Under some rules, specific grounds, such as misconduct of the jury, newly discovered material evidence, or errors of law, are set out that automatically authorize the right to a new trial, see, e. g., Minn. Rules of Proc. 59.01. Under others, the trial court is allowed more discretion and is given the power to grant a new trial motion based on grounds "heretofore recognized," see, e. g., Fed. Rule 59(a). In either case, the discretion granted the judge to set aside the verdict and order a new trial is much greater than on a JNOV motion. In sum, the judge can consider any error of law in the trial that may have prejudiced the movant. The court may take into account prejudicial errors in rulings on the evidence or in the instructions to the jury, evidence of jury or attorney misconduct, newly discovered evidence, or the fact that the verdict is against the weight of the

[*173*]

evidence. This last ground may merit relief even though the legal insufficiency falls short of that required to support a directed verdict or JNOV motion.

The contrast between new trial rulings and a JNOV sometimes appears shadowy, especially when the ground for new trial relates to the sufficiency of the evidence. But the difference is real. The evidence may be such that reasonable people could find as the jury found, precluding a JNOV, but the verdict still may be against the weight of the evidence. Second, the resulting impact of an order granting a JNOV differs sharply from that granting a new trial. The victim of a JNOV is denied the benefit of a favorable jury verdict; the victim of a new trial order complains that he gets too much jury trial, not too little.

The only real limitation imposed on a person moving for a new trial is time. Generally, new trial motions are governed by strict and short timing provisions (i. e., 10 days after the judgment is entered or the verdict is returned). The failure to move within the statutory period is fatal.

The trial judge's decision on a motion for new trial most frequently is controlling. In most judicial systems an immediate appeal cannot be taken from an order granting a new trial as it is interlocutory. This delays appellate review of the new trial order until after the second trial and its verdict, thereby decreasing substantially the likelihood of reversal. If the second proceeding is lacking prejudicial errors, there typically is no justification for disregarding the judgment entered therein simply because the second trial was not necessary. It is difficult to determine which of two reasonable juries was most reasonable. On an appeal from a ruling denying a new trial, the appellate court will reverse only if it finds an abuse of discretion. This seldom occurs on sufficiency of evidence grounds as the appellate court usually defers to the trial judge on the theory that since he was present when the evidence was presented, he is in the best position to determine whether it was substantial.

§ 5–15. Partial and Conditional New Trials

In order to avoid the expense of an entire new trial, the judge may decide to order a new trial only on those issues tainted with error. While a partial new trial may result in considerable savings, it also presents some potential problems. The court must make certain that the issues not retried are truly separable from those resubmitted. Otherwise, the second judgment will remain tainted by the error in the first trial. Indeed, the court probably should not order a partial new trial on liability alone. Jurors' attitudes toward liability frequently are reflected in the amount of damages they award and the issues are so intertwined that if there has been some error concerning the evidence directed toward liability, a new jury should consider both aspects of the case. Thus, most commonly partial new trials are ordered on the amount of damages, not on liability. A minority of courts have argued that partial new trials always are defective as the parties are entitled to a properly instructed and informed jury and, as soon as any prejudicial defect is discovered, the entire first trial is tainted incurably.

Another alternative utilized by judges faced with a new trial motion is to grant the order conditionally. This typically occurs when the challenge to the first proceeding is that the damages awarded by the jury are excessive or inadequate as a matter of law. If the court agrees with that assertion, it may try to avoid the cost of a new trial by stating that it will grant the motion unless the opposing party agrees to a specified reduction or increase in the verdict. Strong arguments against conditional new trial orders have been made on the ground that the judge effectively is supplanting the jury in violation of the parties' rights to a jury trial on the question of damages. By and large these arguments have been unsuccessful. The power to reduce damages (remittitur) is recognized by virtually all judicial systems and has resisted constitutional attack. The power to increase damages (additur) does not exist in the federal courts as it has been held to violate the Seventh Amendment.   Thus, additur exists only in some state courts.   The different treatment accorded remittitur and additur in the federal system does not rest on policy, but rather on the fact that remittitur existed at common law and thus is within the scope of the Amendment. Additur is a more modern device and since it does have an impact on the jury's decision, it is not constitutionally permissible.   The continued vitality of this distinction is doubted by many today.

There are no specific rules governing the amount to be remitted or added.   Different states follow different verbal standards.   However, there are three basic formulations that can be identified.   The judge may reduce or increase the award to the legally sufficient minimum the jury could have awarded, to the maximum that would have been permissible, or he may set the figure between those two extremes at the amount he feels is justified by the evidence.   Once the judge applies one of these standards and sets the figure, the opposing party's decision is simply to accept that figure or go to a new trial.   If the judge's figure is acceptable to the opposing party, the party who originally requested a new trial will find that motion denied and his only option if he is unhappy with the new damage award is to appeal.

§ 5–16. Combined Motions for New Trial and Judgment Notwithstanding the Verdict

In some judicial systems a party may move simultaneously for a JNOV and for a new trial and the judge must rule on both motions. The theory behind requiring concurrent alternative rulings is that it will save time on appeal and will provide further guidance to the appellate court as to why the judge feels the verdict is erroneous. If the motions were bifurcated with the movant seeking and obtaining first a ruling on the JNOV and then a ruling on new trial, a separate appeal would be required from each of those rulings and result in a delay of possibly two years or more before a final decision was reached or a new trial actually begun. Therefore, the trial judge is instructed to rule on both motions simultaneously.

One effect of the joint rulings is to alter some of the normal appealability rules. As is described elsewhere (see § 7–1, infra), most judicial systems authorize appeals only from final judgments. A grant or denial of a JNOV, alone, results in a final judgment being entered. The denial of a new trial motion, alone, also is final as the jury's verdict then is incorporated into a judgment. The grant of a new trial motion is interlocutory, however, as it requires the trial court to begin anew and thus it normally is not immediately appealable. The rules governing joint JNOV-new trial motions alter this fact by providing that if the court grants both the JNOV and the new trial motions, that ruling is appealable immediately. The new trial order is viewed as only an alternative to be used if the JNOV is reversed. If on the initial motion the JNOV is denied and a new trial granted, no immediate appeal lies. See Fed.Rule 50(c), (d).

VI. JUDGMENTS AND THEIR EFFECTS

A. RELIEF FROM JUDGMENTS

§ 6–1. Principles Governing

All judicial systems provide some limited means by which a party may seek to set aside a judgment and obtain a new trial after the time for moving for a new trial or appealing has passed. These provisions are attempts to accommodate the need for finality with the desire to make certain that the truth was found in the original trial. Most commonly, relief is allowed only within certain time periods, usually varying between six months and one year from the entry of the judgment. More rarely, relief is limited only by a reasonable time requirement. Timing restrictions on post judgment relief operate to preserve finality; the certainty produced by finality is merely postponed. The only exception to these rigid time restraints is when the defect in the first proceeding is one going to the very power of the court to try the controversy, as when the court lacked subject matter or personal jurisdiction.

The most common example of cases in which relief is granted is when a default judgment was entered. The due process notion of an effective opportunity to be heard favors adjudications after an adversarial presentation. Thus, the courts treat default relief motions very liberally and will deny relief from those judgments only when it is clear the defendant has no defense to the action or when he has delayed so long that the plaintiff now would be prejudiced by being required to go to trial.

The procedure for setting aside a judgment is to make a motion for relief from the judgment under the appropriate rule. It typically is totally within the trial court's discretion whether to grant or deny relief. The court, in addition to considering whether the reasons alleged for setting aside the judgment are permissible grounds for relief under the applicable rule, usually will take into account other equitable concerns. These may include the prejudice to the opposing party, who may have acted in reliance on the judgment, if the motion is granted, whether the movant has proceeded with due diligence in making the motion, or any other matter that might bear on the fairness of reopening the judgment. The court will not consider whether the first judgment is erroneous, although it may take into account whether opening the judgment and ordering a new trial is likely to produce a different result.

Another method by which a party may seek relief is to bring an independent action to set aside the judgment. This method typically is limited to cases in which the ground for relief is that the judgment in the first proceeding was obtained by fraud. The right to bring an independent action for fraud is an historic one and is limited to charges of extrinsic fraud—fraudulent conduct that prevented the party from discovering evidence or witnesses before trial that could have had substantial impact on the outcome. This approach is seldom utilized.

§ 6–2. Grounds for Relief

Federal Rule 60(b) sets out the most widely recognized grounds for seeking relief. Relief may be granted if the party moves within one year and shows that the judgment was entered due to a mistake, surprise, or excusable neglect, or that some material evidence exists that could not have been discovered earlier, or that the judgment was obtained fraudulently. The courts have not interpreted these grounds very broadly. If mistake or neglect is alleged, gross neglect cannot be found or relief will be denied. Newly discovered evidence may be the subject of a motion for relief only if the evidence was available during the original proceeding. The development of new medical treatments after a damage verdict has been entered in a personal injury suit cannot be presented as newly discovered evidence justifying the reopening of the judgment. The availability of this ground is further limited because the liberal discovery rules present in most jurisdictions make it most difficult to show that evidence that existed at the time of the trial could not have been discovered earlier. In several state systems, a party moving on the basis of fraud is limited to extrinsic fraud on the theory that the trial itself is designed to weed out intrinsic fraud, such as perjury. In this way the judgment winner is protected from being constantly harassed by relief from judgment motions.

A party also may seek relief on the ground that the judgment is void, that it has been satisfied or, in the case of an equitable decree, that the circumstances have changed, or that the law on which the court relied has been reversed, if the motion is made "within a reasonable time." The less rigid time restraints applicable to these grounds for relief reflect the seriousness of the defect being raised and, in some instances, the fact that it would not be possible to discover the ground until more than one year had passed. It is within the court's discretion to decide whether the motion is so untimely as to prejudice the opposing party unduly. Again, however, the grounds listed are rather specific and are interpreted narrowly.

The last ground for relief also is subject only to the reasonable time limitation; it is the catchall clause: "any other reason justifying relief." Although its wording is all embrasive, the courts have applied the clause sparingly to only those

"extraordinary circumstances" demanding re-
dress. Illustratively, the provision has been invoked successfully when a party has failed to comply with a settlement after a dismissal was entered, and when a party failed to appeal a denatural-
ization order or move for relief within a year because he was jailed and denied counsel. The
courts have not used the clause as a vague loop-
hole to circumvent the other time restrictions.

B.   SECURING AND ENFORCING
A JUDGMENT

§ 6–3.   How a Judgment is Enforced

Several judgments are self-enforcing. Judgments declaring the law or quieting title are good
examples. However, other judgments may require the losing party to pay money or to complete some act. In many instances a judgment
winner need not use any enforcement method as
the loser simply will pay the judgment or otherwise comply with the decree. If that is not the
case, the method of enforcing the judgment varies
depending on whether the judgment at issue is
local, that of a sister state, or international in
character.

Enforcement of a local judgment is a purely administrative matter. The judgment winner presents a copy of the judgment to the sheriff and
he issues a writ of execution on property desig-

nated by the judgment creditor. The writ orders any person or corporation controlling the property to turn it over to that officer for the judgment winner. Illustratively, the sheriff may issue a writ garnishing the judgment loser's wages until the judgment has been satisfied. A writ of execution also could be directed at the debtor's automobile and that chattel then would be sold at a judicial sale with the proceeds used to pay the judgment. Any excess proceeds would be returned to the loser. In cases in which the judgment is an injunction, the judgment winner can move to hold the loser in contempt of court for failure to comply with the injunction. If so held, the contemnor may be fined or jailed, depending on the court's discretion.

When an out of state judgment is involved, it becomes necessary to reduce the judgment to a local one before execution. This requires the judgment creditor to bring an action on the judgment in the local court, serving process on the debtor and providing an opportunity to respond. In virtually all instances a local judgment will be entered with enforcement proceeding as just described. This is so because Full Faith and Credit must be given to sister state judgments under the United States Constitution, Article IV, § 1.   Therefore, except for a very limited number of objections, the enforcement court cannot look behind the judgment to reexamine the earlier proceedings. The rationale for requiring the creditor to bring an action on the judgment rather than allowing immediate execution is based on notions of sovereignty. Each state is an independent, sovereign power and cannot directly invade another state's authority over its own residents by enforcing a judgment there. Thus, the procedure defers to the sovereignty of the enforcement state by the form of bringing an action asking those courts to recognize the judgment so that execution may follow. International judgments are treated similarly—an action to enforce must be brought. However, there is no constitutional full faith and credit requirement applicable and the court is given much greater discretion to decide as a matter of comity whether enforcement should take place.

The process of bringing an action on a judgment is often a burdensome formality. Thus, several states have adopted uniform legislation authorizing foreign judgment holders to file the judgment with the local courts and mail a notice to that effect to the judgment debtor. After a short period of time, typically thirty days, in which the debtor can move to vacate, but only on grounds consistent with Full Faith and Credit, the judgment may be executed upon in the same manner as any local court judgment. Uniform Enforcement of Foreign Judgments Act of 1964, 9A Uniform Laws Ann. 488 (1965). The process for enforcing a federal judgment from one state in a federal court in another state is similar, but even simpler. As provided by special statute, 28 U.S. C.A. § 1963, a federal judgment may be registered in another federal court by filing a copy there and upon that act, it will be treated as a local judgment.

§ 6–4. Securing a Judgment—Constitutional Limitations

In some cases the plaintiff may fear that the defendant will transfer all his property to others or outside of the jurisdiction in order to make the enforcement of any judgment, should he lose, very difficult and costly. In order to secure the judgment against this possibility, the plaintiff may request the court to order an attachment or to sequester some of the defendant's assets upon the filing of the action. In this way plaintiff ensures that any judgment obtained will be easily enforceable should defendant refuse to pay.

The process of securing a judgment is accomplished by seeking one of a variety of writs, such as writs of replevin, attachment, garnishment or sequestration. The plaintiff posts a bond, which will be forfeited to the defendant if the suit is found to be frivolous or the attachment solely a means of harassment. The clerk of the court or the judge historically entered the order ex parte and the sheriff seized the property. The defend-

[*187*]

ant received notice only as the seizure took place; he then could appear before the court to ask for relief or to post a bond and obtain possession of his property.

Prejudgment attachments such as just described have come under increasing attack in recent years. They have been successfully challenged as violating the constitutional due process rights of the defendant since no hearing or notice is provided prior to the seizure of the property. See Sniadach v. Family Finance Corp., 395 U.S. 337 (1969). The Supreme Court in a long series of cases has evolved a balancing test by which to test the validity of any prejudgment attachment. The test takes into account the public or governmental interest that would justify postponing the opportunity to be heard—for example, if attachment depends upon a showing that immediate action is necessary as the defendant is likely to transfer or hide the property. Further, the decision to issue such an order must be committed to the discretion of a judicial officer, not merely the clerk of the court. Finally, the debtor must be provided an opportunity to dissolve the writ immediately, with the burden placed on the plaintiff to show why the attachment was justified. See Mitchell v. W. T. Grant Co., 416 U.S. 600 (1974).

One of the open and important questions raised by this line of cases is to what extent they affect

the ability of a court to assert quasi in rem jurisdiction, which necessarily is based on a pre-judg-
ment attachment. Is the desire to assert jurisdiction a sufficient governmental interest to justify the delay of the defendant's due process rights
to a hearing? The Supreme Court has not yet
ruled on this question and the lower courts that
have considered it are divided.

C. THE BINDING EFFECT OF JUDGMENTS

1. IN GENERAL

§ 6–5. The Nomenclature

A complete vocabulary has been developed in
connection with the law on the binding effect of
judgments. Although the courts sometimes mis-
use terms, it is important to understand the
proper terminology in order to understand the
results that may be reached in certain cases.

Res judicata or *claim estoppel* refers to the effect that a final adjudication on the merits of a
cause of action has on an attempt to relitigate the
same cause of action within the same judicial
system. It prevents the relitigation of causes of
action, regardless of what issues actually were
litigated in the first suit. When res judicata is
being asserted against a person who was vic-
torious in the first action, the second judgment is

said to be merged into the first. *Merger* prevents the second action from going forward. When res judicata is asserted against a person who lost the first suit, the second action is said to be barred by the first. *Bar* prevents the second suit from proceeding. When res judicata is being asserted on the basis of a judgment that was entered in a different court system than the present suit, i. e. another state, or the federal court, if the first action was in the state courts, or vice-versa, the judgment is given binding effect because of *Full Faith and Credit*. The Constitution, Art. IV, § 1, and its enabling legislation, 28 U.S.C.A. § 1738, require the second court to give the first judgment the same effect it would have been given in the state where it was rendered. Thus, the law of res judicata as developed in the original forum will govern the binding effect of that judgment in the second court. *Collateral estoppel* or *issue estoppel* is invoked when separate causes of action are presented in the first and second suits. The doctrine provides that any issue that was actually and necessarily litigated in one action will be estopped from being relitigated in a subsequent suit.

Res judicata and collateral estoppel should be distinguished from three other doctrines. *Stare decisis* refers to the policy of the courts to adhere to precedent. Adherence to precedent is the foundation underlying the common law system: it provides the certainty necessary for persons to plan their activities knowing what the governing law is. Stare decisis effect is given only to actual determinations, not dicta. Further, the court has discretion to depart from precedent if it feels the circumstances have changed or that the prior case was decided wrongly. The doctrine of *law of the case* provides that the opinion or judgment of the appellate court on an appeal or writ of error is binding on the lower court when the case is remanded to the trial court for further action. The doctrine arises out of the rule that a final judgment in the highest court is a final determination of the parties' rights. *Election of remedies* is an historic, common law doctrine developed when parties were not allowed to plead alternatively or inconsistently. It provided that once a party chose between several alternative theories of recovery, he had elected his remedy and, should the action fail, could not then sue on any other theory. A few states still invoke the doctrine to bar inconsistent theories of recovery, i. e., to seek reformation, which is premised on the existence of a contract, will preclude a later action for quasi-contract, which assumes no contract exists. However, most courts have abandoned the doctrine.

§ 6–6. General Principles Governing

Res judicata and collateral estoppel both operate with almost total disregard for what the truth is. They are premised on the beliefs that the judicial system cannot tolerate constant relitigation or it will be overburdened; that judgments must be stable and final so that persons will be able to rely on them and plan for the future; and that the judicial system must prevent itself from being used as a tool of harassment. Thus, collateral estoppel precludes the relitigation of the same issues on the assumption that even if the issue was wrongly decided in the first action, the parties had a full and fair opportunity to present their case on that issue and systemic concerns must prevail. Res judicata takes this reasoning one step further. It argues that once the parties have been given a hearing on a cause of action, there can be no relitigation even though there may be some issues that were never introduced or considered in the first action, but that could have had a substantial impact on the outcome. Both doctrines are extremely important tools for planning litigation as the cautious attorney must take care to frame the case so as not to be precluded in a later action, should a subsequent suit be desirable.

Since res judicata and collateral estoppel are judicial doctrines, it is necessary to check in the jurisdiction where suit is brought to determine how rigidly the courts there enforce these restraints. There is considerable variation. A general description follows. The reader is advised for more comprehensive treatment to refer to R. Casad, *Res Judicata in a Nutshell* (1976).

2. RES JUDICATA

§ 6-7. Standard for Asserting

A party asserting res judicata must show that the *same cause of action* or *same claim* is involved in both suits, that there was a *final judgment* on that cause of action and, in most jurisdictions, that the prior judgment was *on the merits*. As is discussed in the next section, the major problem in applying this standard has been in defining what constitutes a single claim or cause of action. Finality, for res judicata purposes, "represents the completion of all steps in the adjudication of a claim by the court, short of execution." American Law Institute, Restatement, Second, Judgments § 41 (Tent. Draft No. 2 1975). Thus, finality generally is not affected by the taking of an appeal, unless the appellate court vacates the judgment and orders a trial de novo. The court in a second proceeding may stay the action until the appeal from the first judgment is prosecuted. While that is the sounder approach, the court has discretion simply to apply res judicata and dismiss the suit based on the first trial court's judgment.

A judgment involving the same cause of action may be final, but still not preclude a second action if it is not on the merits. For example, a dismissal for lack of subject matter jurisdiction will not bar the identical action from being brought in a court having proper jurisdiction. The requirement of a judgment on the merits has produced some problems with pretrial dismissals that bear closely on the merits. Courts do not agree on how to treat demurrers or dismissals for failure to state a claim for relief for res judicata purposes. It is clear that if the pleader merely restates the same complaint in another action, res judicata will apply. Some courts have overruled res judicata challenges when the second complaint alleges other facts or theories, arguing that the merits never were actually considered in the first action. Other courts handle this problem by granting the plaintiff a right to amend at the time of the first dismissal. If he fails to do so or fails to appeal, then res judicata will apply. This approach is particularly prevalent in systems, such as the federal courts, that have very liberal pleading rules and that permit pretrial dismissals on the pleadings only when there is no conceivable theory on which the plaintiff could base his case.

Another problem that has arisen is how to treat involuntary dismissals entered for failure to prosecute or for failure to comply with some court order. The rules governing these dismissals typically provide that they will be with prejudice unless otherwise ordered, see, e. g., Fed.Rule 41(b). Thus, the question presented is whether they should be given res judicata effect even though it is clear by the very nature of the dismissal that the merits of the case never were reached. The weight of authority applies res judicata, noting that the availability of motions for relief from judgment and appeal ameliorates the harshness of this decision. Other courts refuse res judicata effect on the ground that the dismissal is not on the merits.

In order to avoid the kinds of problems discussed above, the ALI Restatement, Second, Judgments § 48 (Tent. Draft No. 2 1975), omits entirely the phrase "on the merits" from its definition of bar. Instead, the question whether preclusive effect should be given to these dismissals is determined as a matter of sound judicial administration and by considering the fairness to the defendant if a second action is allowed. Both of these concerns require that the litigation terminate after the first dismissal and the question whether the court's decision involved the merits is irrelevant.

§ 6–8. What is a Cause of Action

The particular test that a court adopts defining cause of action (or claim) may be heavily influenced by several outside considerations. Some courts utilize a very broad test in keeping with the policies of their system to encourage the broadest possible joinder of claims and defenses in the first suit and thereby avoid multiple suits.

Others invoke a very narrow conception because they are concerned about the harshness of the doctrine and prefer to rely on collateral estoppel to prevent duplicative litigation. Yet others may be influenced by the merits of the claim of the party opposing the assertion of res judicata and thus define the cause of action most narrowly to allow him to present his case. A few courts appear to take into account whether the cause of action was split intentionally. What follows is a description of the various tests utilized. However, the attorney should be aware, after determining which test is used in the forum court, that the court may be swayed by the other factors just mentioned.

The narrowest conception of cause of action looks to the *rights* that allegedly have been violated. Separate causes of action are involved when more than one right was infringed, even though the several rights involved were impinged upon by a single act. Some courts adhering to the "right" test have phrased the standard in terms of an inquiry into whether a second judgment could upset the first. In practice the test often will depend on history and whether the allegations presented would have been raised in different forms of action. For example, personal injury and car damages arising from the same accident present different causes of action under this test because one involves trespass to the person, the other trespass to a chattel. However, back injuries and neurological damage constitute the violation of one right—trespass to person. Actions involving separate pieces of property also involve different rights. Res judicata will be applied in contract disputes depending on whether the contract is deemed indivisible or divisible, providing for separate rights.

Most courts do not adhere to the "right" definition of cause of action as it is a product of the common law writ system when cases could consist only of a single issue. While it was necessary then to protect parties from preclusion since they could not have raised multiple causes in one suit, modern claim joinder affords that opportunity and suggests that a broader res judicata test be utilized. Thus, cause of action is defined more often in terms of how many *wrongs* were committed, focusing on the defendant's acts, rather than the plaintiff's injuries. One tortious act constitutes one cause of action even though it may have produced a series of injuries to person and property. In actions based on violations of property or contract rights, the focus will be on the acts of the defendant that produced injury or served to breach.

The broadest test for the assertion of res judicata is the transaction test, proposed in ALI, Restatement, Second, Judgments § 61 (Tent. Draft No. 1 1973). Under the test any acts or series of occurrences that may have produced an injury or series of injuries should be presented in a single suit. The obvious effect of this approach is to create compulsory joinder of claims in the first action. Thus, there has been some resistance to the transaction standard on the ground that if the pleading and joinder rules are permissive only (see § 3–18, supra), then it is unfair and improper for the courts to create a compulsory joinder system indirectly through the device of res judicata.

Both the "right" and the "wrong" test for cause of action necessitate not only that the same parties or their privies be involved in both suits, see § 6–9, infra, but also that the parties remain in essentially the same offensive-defensive posture in both actions. In an action between A and B, those tests look to how many of A's rights were violated or how many wrongful acts were committed by B. If B also has a potential claim against A arising out of the same series of events, that will constitute a separate cause of action as it will require an inquiry into B's rights and A's wrongful acts. The transaction test does not recognize this distinction and res judicata would apply to both A's claims and B's claims under that standard.

Defining cause of action in terms of whose rights or wrongs are involved has caused some problems when applied in situations in which the same facts may be asserted by B as an affirmative defense or as a counterclaim. The judicial economy and harassment rationales underlying the application of res judicata suggest that B should be compelled to raise both the defense and the counterclaim in the first suit. This would mean that even if B defaults res judicata should bar another action by B against A, as B had the opportunity to raise the defense and the counterclaim was merged into the defense. Most courts have not gone so far. A distinction is drawn between omitted and litigated defenses, with res judicata being applied in a subsequent suit by B against A only if B asserted a defense, but failed to include the counterclaim. The focus in determining whether B has split the cause of action is whether the same facts are in issue and the same evidence will be utilized for both the defense and the omitted claim. Some courts have not gone even that far; they have applied the same evidence test in such a way (i. e., pointing to new evidence on damages, not germane to the defense) that res judicata cannot ever be invoked successfully in this situation.

§ 6–9. Who Will be Bound

The doctrine of res judicata is applicable only when the second action is between persons who were parties or who are in privity with persons who were parties in the first action. When new parties are involved in the second action, a separate or different cause of action is presented. If any preclusive effect is to attach to the first judgment, it will be through the application of collateral estoppel, not res judicata. Thus, the question of who will be bound by res judicata often depends upon the definition of privies.

Historically, a person who was in privity with a party was one who acquired an interest in the subject matter of the suit after it had been brought. Successors in interest, whether they obtained their interests by virtue of an assignment, by inheritance or by law were treated as parties for res judicata purposes. Modern courts have extended privity concepts to a larger number of circumstances. For example, privity has been held to embrace employer-employee and indemnitor-indemnitee relationships. Indeed, persons whose liability, if any, is derivative have been held in privity with those from whom their liability derives. Additionally, if a person actually controls the first suit, he will be found to be in privity with the named parties to that suit. Appointed or legal representatives, such as guardians or administrators, are in privity with the person whom they are representing. While this listing of privity relationships is not exhaustive, it illustrates the modern trend to expand the scope of res judicata to bind persons whose interests are so wedded to those of existing parties that it would be a waste of judicial effort to allow a second action simply because they were not named in the first suit. However, because res judicata effects are so drastic—precluding issues that ought to have been litigated, as well as those that actually were litigated—courts still refuse to extend privity to embrace persons having similar, or even identical, interests if there is no special relationship existing between those individuals. The focus is on the type of relationship between the party and the alleged privy, as well as their identity of interest in light of that relationship.

§ 6–10. Policies Outweighing Res Judicata

There are some circumstances in which even though the standard for applying res judicata has been met, preclusion will not result. These situations arise when the judicial economy policies fostered by res judicata are outweighed by some other public policy underlying the type of action that is involved. Illustratively, in a suit involving the sale of land in which both the buyer and the seller were seeking title, a court overruled all res judicata objections since to hold otherwise would be inequitable and would result in an unclear title. The policies underlying the transfer of property required that some solution be given the parties. Adams v. Pearson, 104 N.E.2d 267 (Ill.1952). In another action res judicata was outweighed by the policies underlying the workmen's compensation act so that a prior common law negligence action did not preclude the statutory remedy, it only reduced the judgment therein. Varsity Amusement Co. v. Butters, 394 P.2d 603 (Colo.1964).

3. COLLATERAL ESTOPPEL

§ 6–11. Standard for Asserting

In order for collateral estoppel to be invoked successfully, the party asserting estoppel must show that the same or *identical issue* is presented in Action–2 that was decided in Action–1, and that the issue was *actually* and *necessarily* decided in the first suit. The presence of each element of this test assures that preclusion will result only after a party has had a full opportunity to prove a given issue. Conversely, judicial economy becomes paramount when this assurance exists.

The requirement of identical issues is met easily when the plaintiff is asserting several claims based on a single wrongful act of the defendant. The question whether the defendant acted negligently in driving his automobile will be the same in a suit claiming damages for personal injuries to the driver as in a later suit by the driver's spouse for loss of consortium. However, in actions arising out of acts that occurred at different times, the issues though similar, necessarily are not identical. For example, a suit in 1977 to establish the taxability of an organization claiming a tax exemption as a religious group will have no preclusive effect on a similar action in 1978. A finding that the defendant does or does not function as a religious organization in 1977 will not be given collateral estoppel effect as the character of the defendant's activities in 1978 may have changed—the issue is not identical. Similarly, collateral estoppel will not be available in successive actions on separate bonds or negotiable instruments in which the same defense—whether the plaintiff purchased the bonds for value—is raised. The issues are not identical; the proof that the plaintiff was or was not a bona fide purchaser of one bond, does not prove how he obtained any of the other bonds.

The above situations are the most common set of circumstances in which the lack of an identical issue precludes collateral estoppel. A few courts have gone even further and have ruled that identical issues are not present when the issue is raised in the first action by way of defense and in the second action as part of a claim. Under this approach, the issue whether a plaintiff is free from contributory negligence is not identical to the issue whether the plaintiff was negligent. These courts are applying the identity of issues test literally, focusing on the fact that different burdens of proof are applicable to the issue in each action so that it is not identical. Most courts have not gone so far and have given collateral estoppel effect to these issues, at least when the burden of proof was greater in the first action than in the second.

A question whether an issue was actually litigated arises when a general verdict is rendered and the judgment could be based on findings on one or more issues in the case. The minority view is that in such cases the court in the second action is to treat all issues as actually litigated, giving a very broad collateral estoppel effect to the judgment. The majority view is that when the judgment in the first action may have been based on findings on more than one issue, no collateral estoppel effect will be given to any issue in the case unless evidence is introduced showing which issues actually were decided. As a further limitation, only extrinsic evidence that supports the verdict is allowed; the evidence cannot contradict the verdict. For example, consider an action in which A sues B for injuries caused by B's negligence. B alleges as a defense that A was contributorily negligent. There is a general verdict for B. That verdict could be based on a finding that A was contributorily negligent, that B was free from negligence, or both. B can assert collateral estoppel in a subsequent suit against A only if she can show on what the jury rested its verdict. However, under no circumstances can A introduce evidence to the effect that his alleged contributory negligence was not actually litigated or considered by the jury, as that would contradict the verdict.

The third requirement for asserting collateral estoppel—whether the issue was necessary to the first proceeding—has posed great difficulty for the courts. This requirement assures that the parties vigorously litigated the issue so that it is fair to prevent its relitigation in a second action because there is little likelihood that the results will be different the second time around. The courts have developed a few general rules to aid in this inquiry. Facts found against the prevailing party in the first action are deemed unnecessary. The prevailing party has no incentive to appeal and thus the issue will not be given collateral estoppel effect as vigorous prosecution on that issue is not assured. On the other hand, alternative holdings are given full collateral estoppel effect; there is no need to determine which finding was necessary to the judgment. It is assumed that one issue is no less necessary than the other. Thus, for example, in the negligence hypothetical above, if a special verdict had been rendered specifically finding A contributorily negligent and B free from negligence, B could assert collateral estoppel against A on both those issues. Interestingly, the Restatement, Second, Judgments § 68 (Tent. Draft No. 1 1973), advocates that no collateral estoppel effect be given in this situ-

ation because of a concern that this broad
approach will encourage appeals. However, if
the parties have appealed and the appellate court
affirms the alternative findings, then the Restatement would apply collateral estoppel to those
issues.

§ 6-12. Mediate and Ultimate Facts

Another method utilized by the courts to determine when to uphold the assertion of collateral
estoppel was to distinguish between mediate and
ultimate facts. Ultimate facts were those on
which the case was based—i. e., does plaintiff have
title. Mediate facts were those that provided the
means by which the court could reach a conclusion on the ultimate facts—i. e., did plaintiff obtain title through a fraudulent scheme. Concerns
over how to prove whether a mediate fact actually was litigated led to a rule that mediate facts
would not be given collateral estoppel effect. Another concern prompting the use of the mediate/
ultimate fact distinction was the problem of foreseeability. This concern was particularly prevalent when a fact found in the first action,
whether mediate or ultimate there, was only a
mediate fact in the second action. Courts refused
collateral estoppel effect under those circumstances in order to protect against surprise to the losing litigant who, it was assumed, could not have
foreseen all the possible mediate facts that might

rest on a given issue and thus may not have litigated it fully the first time.

The mediate/ultimate fact distinction is largely of historic significance. The availability of devices such as special verdicts and general verdicts with interrogatories has eroded the need for this rule. See § 5–10, supra. The Restatement, Second, Judgments § 68 (Tent. Draft No. 1 1973), states that the modern approach is to determine whether the fact issue on which collateral estoppel is being asserted was necessary and important, rather than merely evidentiary, in the first suit. If so and the issue was actually litigated, then it is fair to apply collateral estoppel. There is no need to be concerned with foreseeability as the parties had incentive to vigorously litigate the issue in the first proceeding.

§ 6–13. Who Will be Bound

Historically, the question of who could benefit from or who would be bound by collateral estoppel was treated the same way as when res judicata was involved: only parties and their privies could invoke or be precluded by estoppel. See § 6–9, supra. This approach necessarily narrowed the scope of collateral estoppel. Even though an issue could be identical in two different actions and judicial economy concerns would support preventing its relitigation in a second action, collateral estoppel effect was denied. The reasoning supporting this restriction was twofold. In cases in which collateral estoppel is asserted against someone who was not a party to the first action, due process prevents its application as the non-party must be given an opportunity to be heard. The doctrine of mutuality prevented the successful assertion of collateral estoppel by a non-party against someone who did litigate the first suit. That doctrine is premised on the notion that everyone should be treated equally. Since a party to an action cannot assert collateral estoppel against someone who was not a party to that suit, neither should the non-party be allowed to assert estoppel against him. In this way mutuality operated in favor of someone who had been heard giving that person a second chance to prove the issue in his favor.

While due process continues to prevent the assertion of collateral estoppel against one who was not a party to the first suit, the question whether mutuality is a necessary limitation on the scope of collateral estoppel is debatable. Mutuality has been abandoned in about half the jurisdictions, following the lead of California in Bernhard v. Bank of America Nat. Trust & Sav. Ass'n, 122 P.2d 892 (Cal.1942). Those courts who have abandoned the doctrine argue that a person should not be allowed to continuously litigate a fruitless claim, particularly when relitigation is unlikely to change the result. The proper focus in determining whether a non-party can assert collateral estoppel against a party is whether the party had a full and fair opportunity to litigate the issue in the first action. Of course, the issues must be identical in both suits.

Courts have abandoned mutuality in varying degrees. The most commonly recognized situation is when the person asserting collateral estoppel is doing so defensively. In those cases judicial economy concerns are great because it appears that the party to the first suit may simply be suing seriatim. Further, there is a desire to protect the new defendant from such harassing litigation. The problem becomes more difficult when collateral estoppel is being asserted offensively— when a non-party is attempting to take advantage of a judgment that is adverse to a party in the first suit. Certainly, there is less need to be concerned about the new party, and there is a much greater concern about the defendant. Did he foresee this second suit at the time of the first action so that he had the incentive to litigate that suit fully? Some courts have refused to allow collateral estoppel to be asserted offensively by a non-party. Others have allowed the assertion when it is against someone who was the aggressor in the first suit, but not when it is against someone who was a defendant in the first suit. This distinction is based on the notion that the defending party to the first action necessarily was at a disadvantage in that suit and to make certain that he had a fair opportunity to be heard, collateral estoppel should not be applied. A few courts have refused to reject collateral estoppel merely because of the posture of the parties. Instead, they focus on whether the party to both actions could have foreseen the second suit. If so, the burden shifts to that party to show that he did not fully litigate the issue in the first action. If that is not shown, collateral estoppel will be applied.

In a recent decision the United States Supreme Court authorized the offensive use of collateral estoppel in the federal courts in federal question cases. Parklane Hosiery Co. v. Shore, 99 S.Ct. 645 (1979). The Court ruled that the trial court had broad discretion to determine this question and that collateral estoppel should be applied unless the court finds that the plaintiff easily could have joined in the first action or that its application of collateral estoppel would be unfair to the defendant. The federal standard thus looks not only to foreseeability, but also to other potential unfairness and it seeks not to reward a plaintiff who chose not to join in the first suit in order not to be bound by that judgment, if it were for the defendant. The majority of state courts have not gone so far.

§ 6–14. Limitations on the Application of Collateral Estoppel

The availability of collateral estoppel may be limited by substantial policies outweighing the desire for judicial economy and certainty. For example, it was argued that the doctrine could not be invoked when to do so would effectively deny the opposing party a right to a jury trial on that issue as the first suit was tried without a jury. The Supreme Court recently rejected this argument, however, ruling that an equitable determination can have collateral estoppel effect in a subsequent legal action without violating the Seventh Amendment. Parklane Hosiery Co. v. Shore, 99 S.Ct. 645 (1979).

Another limitation on the application of collateral estoppel arises when the first action was before a court of limited jurisdiction. The courts are divided on the question whether to give collateral estoppel to issues when the claims raised in the second action were outside the jurisdictional power of the first court. The question becomes even more acute when the second court has exclusive jurisdiction. This question has arisen in antitrust and patent cases in the federal courts when there have been prior state proceedings in which those courts have ruled on issues of antitrust violations or patent validity in the course of deciding whether a contract was illegal or wheth-

er royalties were due under a licensing arrange-
ment. In the antitrust cases, the courts have
ruled that the punitive and exclusive nature of
the federal remedy precludes collateral estoppel.
Lyons v. Westinghouse Elec. Corp., 222 F.2d 184
(2d Cir. 1955). In patent cases the courts have
allowed collateral estoppel to be applied as to any
of the underlying facts and have refrained from
giving collateral estoppel only to the "congerie
of facts" establishing the issue of patent validity
or infringement. Becher v. Contoure Labs., Inc.,
279 U.S. 388 (1929). In this way they avoid duplicative relitigation, but protect their exclusive
right to rule on the patent itself.

The final limitation on the application of collateral estoppel arises because of changes in the
law that occur between the first and second actions. If the law is altered to change the operative facts necessary to obtain a favorable ruling,
then collateral estoppel will not apply. To hold
otherwise would result in unequal treatment being afforded persons under the law simply because
of the fortuity of a person obtaining a prior ruling. For example, A brings a tax refund action
on the theory that an assignment of royalties under a 1928 patent licensing agreement to his wife
B was valid so that income under that agreement
during the years 1929–1931 was not taxable to
him. The court finds that the assignment is valid
and thus that A is not liable for tax on those roy-

alties, but is due a refund. The law changes as to what must be shown to constitute a valid assignment between husband and wife. Collateral estoppel will not be available to A in a refund suit for taxes collected on royalties earned from 1937–41 on the issue of whether there has been a valid assignment, new additional evidence must be introduced. Commissioner v. Sunnen, 333 U.S. 591 (1948). The need for tax equality outweighs the policies underlying collateral estoppel.

VII. APPEALS

A. TIME FOR BRINGING AN APPEAL

1. THE FINAL JUDGMENT RULE

§ 7–1. Final Judgment Rule

Most jurisdictions authorize an appeal only from the entry of a final judgment in the action. The final judgment is defined as that order that leaves nothing to be done in the action except to execute on the judgment. It concludes all the rights that were subject to litigation. For example, an order dismissing a juror for cause, though conclusive on that question, is not a final judgment as the rights that are the subject of the action have not been decided. If the attorney objects to the ruling, he may raise his objection on appeal, but must wait to take an appeal until a judgment is entered. This type of order commonly is described as reviewable, but not appealable. The only exceptions to the final judgment rule are incorporated in specific statutes, see § 7–3, infra, or in a few well-recognized judicial doctrines, see § 7–4, infra.

The rationale supporting the final judgment rule is severalfold. In part it stems from a desire to obtain judicial economy—a single appeal in which all objections to the trial court's rulings are raised should be more efficient than several appeals, each requiring its own set of briefs, records, oral argument, and opinions. Indeed, the need for an appeal on a given ruling may be avoided totally if the losing party on that issue ultimately prevails in the trial court. Appeals from final judgments also avoid the problem of delaying the trial in order to decide interlocutory matters. This further protects against the possibility that an appeal may be used to harass the opposing party.

A few jurisdictions, such as New York, have rejected the final judgment rule and are very permissive about allowing immediate appeals from any trial court order. These jurisdictions focus on the fact that an immediate appeal may avoid an unnecessary trial, if the question is one that will decide whether the suit should proceed. Alternatively, an immediate appeal may result in a better trial as all preliminary issues will be fully resolved. Further, the final judgment rule effectively prevents some orders from ever being reviewed because they do not affect the merits and will not be deemed prejudicial enough to merit review after the trial is completed. The absence of appellate guidance on these matters can result in inconsistent treatment by the lower courts. Allowing interlocutory appeals on all preliminary orders assures the appellate courts the opportunity to fulfill their function of establishing uniform law.

Thus, there are persuasive arguments supporting and criticizing the final judgment rule. The important thing to be aware of is whether the jurisdiction in which suit is filed adheres to the rule. If it does not, then failure to take an immediate appeal will waive the right to raise that issue on an appeal from the final judgment.

§ 7-2. Specialized Rules for Multi-claim, Multi-party Cases

The application of the final judgment rule in multi-claim, multi-party litigation has posed some problems when the trial court reaches a final decision on some of the claims before it is ready to render a judgment on the entire action. Postponing an appeal until all the claims have been decided may result in an unnecessary delay on a claim that has been fully and finally determined. Thus, special rules have been developed for identifying those orders in multi-claim, multi-party disputes that determine finally the action as it pertains to a given party or claim in order to allow an immediate appeal in those situations. These provisions are not exceptions to the final judgment rule. Rather, they represent standards for applying that rule in those contexts.

A good example is Federal Rule 54(b). Under that rule, in an action having multiple claims or parties, the trial court identifies its order as appealable by making an express direction for the entry of a judgment on the claim involved and by certifying that there is no just reason to delay the appeal. In the absence of this two part certification, the appellate court will dismiss the appeal as violative of the final judgment rule. If the certification is present, the appellate court may review the decision of the trial court that there was no just reason to delay the appeal, utilizing an abuse of discretion standard. It also may consider de novo whether in fact more than one claim is present in the suit or whether the court merely ruled on one of the alternative theories on which the plaintiff's single claim was based.

Both of these questions have caused some difficulties for the trial and appellate courts. When multiple parties are present multiple claims may be easily identified. In two party disputes the standard exercised is that multiple claims are present if each theory presented is one that could have been separately and concurrently enforced. In general, courts are agreed that only the infrequent, harsh case merits a finding that there is no just reason for delay. The court must balance whether the appeal could simplify the trial or whether it would result in a double review of many of the same issues after a judgment is reached on the remaining claims. Similarly, it may weigh the immediate benefit of a recovery to the winning party on the earlier appeal against the possibility that the judgment on one claim should be stayed because it may be set-off by a judgment for the opposing party on the remaining claims.

2. EXCEPTIONS TO THE FINAL JUDGMENT RULE

§ 7–3. Statutory Interlocutory Appeals Routes

A brief examination of the federal interlocutory appeals statutes provides a good illustration of the types of exceptions that typically are recognized in systems observing the final judgment rule.

In one statute, 28 U.S.C.A. § 1292(b), a procedure for discretionary interlocutory appeals is provided requiring the trial court and the appellate court both to certify that the order should be appealed immediately. The standard for certification is that the issue involves a "controlling question of law," that there is "substantial ground for difference of opinion" on that issue, and that an immediate appeal may "materially advance the ultimate termination of the litigation." The purpose of this appeals route is to allow immediate review of important questions. By requiring certification at both levels, the trial court, which is most familiar with the entire proceeding, can pass on whether the appellant raises a crucial issue or is appealing as a dilatory tactic. The appellate court can estimate better its own burdens and can make its decision on appealability relatively free from pressures by the litigants. The standard rests heavily on the discretion of both courts as there may be considerable differences of opinion as to whether any given issue is controlling or as to what will aid the early termination of the suit.

The other statutory appeals measure is embodied in 28 U.S.C.A. § 1292(a). That provision sets out specific categories of orders or types of proceedings from which an interlocutory appeal is permissible. It lists four categories: (1) orders "granting, continuing, modifying, refusing or dissolving injunctions, or refusing to dissolve or modify injunctions"; (2) orders involving receiverships; (3) interlocutory decrees in admiralty cases; and (4) judgments in patent infringement suits that are final except for an accounting. Each one of these exceptions is quite concrete and represents a decision based on concerns that in these areas immediacy is terribly important. Analogous state provisions may delineate other orders that are perceived as demanding immediate appellate review. For example, Minnesota includes a right of appeal to the state Supreme Court from an order vacating or sustaining an attachment. Minn.R.Civ.App. § 103.03(c).

§ 7-4. Judicial Interlocutory Appeals Routes

There are a few well-recognized judicial exceptions to the final judgment rule by which the courts will allow an appeal even though portions of the case remain undecided. The most famous of these is the *collateral order doctrine*. Under

the collateral order doctrine an immediate appeal
may be taken from an order that is final and unrelated to the merits (collateral) but that, if it is
not appealed immediately, may result in irreparable damage to the appellant.   Cohen v. Beneficial
Industrial Loan Corp., 337 U.S. 541 (1949).   The
appellate court determines whether this standard
has been met when the appeal is filed.

Determining whether an order is collateral has
not posed too much difficulty for the courts.
Many orders are clearly unrelated to the merits.
Those that are separate, but more closely intertwined also may meet the standard.   However,
in those cases the courts place much greater
emphasis on the irreparable harm portion of the
standard.   What constitutes irreparable harm is
within the court's discretion.   In large measure
the court will focus on the severity of the potential
injury, the probability of harm occurring, and the
likelihood that review would be ineffective if it
were delayed.   Examples of some orders that have
been held within the collateral order doctrine are:
the denial of a motion to impose security for costs
on plaintiffs in a shareholder derivative suit; the
denial of a motion to proceed in forma pauperis;
and the grant of a motion to require the plaintiff
in a class action to send individual notice to all
the unnamed class members.

In the federal class action area an off-shoot of
the collateral order doctrine was developed termed

the *death knell doctrine*. Orders denying class certification are not truly collateral in the sense that the certification process often requires some inquiry into the merits of the claims involved, if only to examine what common questions are involved. Also, they are not final as the court is directed to consider their revision throughout the trial. However, in many class suits the individual members each have only very small claims and it would not be feasible to bring the action except as a class suit, so that denial of class certification may result as a practical matter in ending the litigation. In response to this problem, the Second Circuit developed the death knell doctrine allowing an immediate appeal under these circumstances on the theory that the denial was effectively a final order collateral to the merits that if not appealable would result in the death of the action, irreparably harming the plaintiffs. Eisen v. Carlisle & Jacquelin, 370 F.2d 119 (2d Cir. 1966). An appeal also was authorized from an order granting class certification on what was termed an "inverse death knell theory." Herbst v. International Tel. & Tel. Corp., 495 F.2d 1308 (2d Cir. 1974). The Supreme Court recently rejected the death knell doctrine (and by implication the inverse death knell doctrine). It ruled that the doctrine violated the final judgment rule and insofar as it rested on the peculiar nature of class actions, the decision to allow an appeal was a legislative one. Coopers & Lybrand v. Livesay, 98 S.Ct. 2454 (1978).

Another judicial interlocutory appeals route authorizes the appellate court to allow an appeal from a non-final decision having *irremediable consequences.* The device was first invoked by the Supreme Court in Forgay v. Conrad, 6 How. (47 U.S.) 201 (1848). In that case, the district court made a partial adjudication of a claim, but ordered the losing party to deliver the physical property involved to the opponent immediately. In that way it treated its partial ruling as final. The appellate court allowed the appeal to avoid the potentially irreparable harm that would occur to the losing party in the absence of immediate review. The courts have used this irremediable consequences rationale very seldom, but it does represent an exception created to provide justice when the application of the final judgment rule would operate very harshly.

§ 7–5. Extraordinary Routes of Appeal

There are two extraordinary routes of appeal that must be mentioned, though they are of limited use. The first is an application to the appellate court for a *writ of mandamus* ordering the trial court to reverse its ruling. Mandamus is based on the theory that the trial court has abused its discretion to such a degree that the appellate court must consider the question immediately. It typically can be used successfully only in extreme cases as it represents a deliberate and direct interference with the trial court during the course of a trial. For example, mandamus was held proper when the appellate court found that the judge had totally abdicated his judicial function by essentially allowing a case to be decided by a master. La Buy v. Howes Leather Co., 352 U.S. 249 (1957). It also was used to review Judge Sirica's ruling on the discoverability of the presidential tapes because of the public interest in ending the controversy over that issue as soon as possible. Nixon v. Sirica, 487 F.2d 700 (D.C.Cir. 1973).

While mandamus typically is utilized only in extraordinary circumstances, a few states have made greater use of that appeals route to provide for immediate review of certain issues. Illustratively, in California rulings denying motions to quash service of process on the ground of lack of personal jurisdiction must be appealed immediately by an application for mandamus. This use of mandamus is so deeply ensconced that failure to so act results in a waiver of the objection and personal jurisdiction cannot be raised on a later appeal from the final judgment.

Another extraordinary route of appeal that should be noted is *contempt*. This method most commonly is available when discovery orders are involved. Failure to obey the court's order will result in the disobedient party being held in contempt. A contempt judgment is a final judgment and may be appealed immediately. This method of appeal necessarily is very risky since if the appellate court affirms the lower court's discovery order, the contempt judgment will stand. Further, only criminal contempt is immediately appealable so that if the court determines that the party was adjudged in civil contempt, an appeal may not be allowed and the contempt judgment will remain. The difference between civil and criminal contempt is discussed elsewhere. Suffice it to say it depends on the nature of the proceeding and the type of sentence imposed. See D. Dobbs, *Remedies* 96 (1973). Despite these risks, in some cases this method has been utilized to avoid the delay that would result in adhering to the final judgment rule in the main action.

B. THE MECHANICS OF APPEAL

§ 7–6. Appealable Issues

While it might seem obvious that the losing party can appeal adverse findings, the rules concerning what issues can be raised on appeal or cross-appeal are somewhat more complex. To begin with, only rulings that were objected to below may be presented by the appellant. Losing parties may appeal all adverse rulings to which they objected. However, winning parties may not appeal from findings deemed erroneous if those findings are not necessary to the decree. The rationale for this restriction is that unnecessary findings will not be the basis for collateral estoppel and thus there is no need for the appeal as no prejudice will result to the winning party by denying it.

On the other hand, if the losing party appeals, the appellee may raise in response any issue that would sustain the judgment, whether or not it was decided below. The basic question in deciding whether the appellee can raise new grounds sustaining the judgment is one of fairness: is the case in the same basic posture it would have been had the issue been introduced below. The appellee is limited to raising issues in support of the judgment, unless he files a cross-appeal. This is particularly important in the third-party context. Assume A sues B for personal injuries and B joins C, his insurer, as a third-party defendant based on an indemnity theory. A loses and the claim against C is dismissed as no right to indemnity arose. A appeals. If B wants to preserve his right to indemnity in the event of a reversal, he must cross-appeal against C, he cannot merely raise that issue by way of his responsive brief.

VIII. SPECIALIZED MULTI–PARTY–MULTI–CLAIM PROCEEDINGS

A. CLASS ACTIONS

§ 8–1. General Purpose and Utility of Class Actions

The class action device allows one or more persons to sue or be sued on behalf of themselves and other individuals who allegedly possess similar grievances or have been harmed in a similar way. The action is permitted to be brought in a representative fashion in order to allow the assertion of legal rights in situations in which the numbers of people involved and, in some instances, the small individual amounts involved, otherwise effectively would prevent the vindication of those rights. Further, the device is an efficient and economical means for the courts and the parties to try a case in which there are common interests. Thus, class suits serve several important objectives.

Current opinion is greatly divided as to the actual utility of class actions. Critics point to the fact that many of the suits filed in the last few years have been extremely burdensome, costly and time-consuming, and only a few have reached judgment. Further, class action filings have increased dramatically, to a point at which it is argued that they have become strike suits, filed by attorneys seeking fat fees but producing few other real benefits. It also is noted that the large, complex modern class suit alters our concept of the adversary system. This is shown in two ways. First, the judge's role changes from a passive one to a very active one. This is necessitated by the fact that the judge must oversee the proceedings very carefully to make certain that the rights of the absent class members are being protected. He cannot rely on the named representative or counsel because at various points their interests may diverge from the other class members. Additionally, the complexity of the action requires the judge to act in many instances as an administrator, devising notice schemes and methods of computing and distributing damages. The second major change produced by class actions is that they have thrust the courts into the policy arena. In the traditional two party suit, the court has little overt concern for the creation of law and the focus is on the specific, local problem before it. Class suits force the courts to deal with public policy questions, rather than leaving those issues to the executive or the legislature. The very numbers of persons involved reflect the fact that the policy or law being sued upon has peculiar public interest. Further, class actions litigants often function as private attorneys' general forcing adherence to or changes in the law by the very impact of their actions.

These criticisms do not suggest that class suits be abandoned; they do point to some issues that must be faced in the near future in order to better regulate abuses and problem areas. At present, when the debate is so alive, an individual court's application of rule requirements or willingness to adopt new management procedures often is influenced by its feelings as to whether class action critics or advocates present the true situation.

§ 8-2. Types of Class Action Statutes

There are basically five different types of class action statutes in the United States today. A brief look at those provisions will illustrate some of the concerns relevant under each approach.

A few states have class action rules modelled on the original equity rules. They allow class suits when joinder of all the members is not feasible and there is adequate representation of their interests. No further guidance is given to the courts. The major limitation is that class suits are authorized only in equity, which means they are not available when damages are being sought.

Similar to the equity approach is that followed by those states having the Field Code as their procedural rules. In those states the same minimum requirements of impracticable joinder and adequacy of representation control, but class actions are available in law and in equity. Further, common questions must be shared by the class members. Courts frequently interpret the code requirements as necessitating that there be an ascertainable class and that the class possess a community of interest. In looking at these two requirements the court essentially will consider whether the individual class members will be identifiable, at least at the damage stage, the number of common questions that exist as compared to the individual issues that will have to be litigated, and, at least to some degree, the social utility of the action. The test is a balancing one, with the court weighing the economies to be gained by allowing the action to proceed against concerns of adequacy of representation and cohesiveness of interest on the part of the class.

Another class action rule is the 1938 federal provision, Fed.Rule 23, which although it no longer is used in the federal courts is followed in several states. Under that approach the same requirements of impracticable joinder, common questions and adequacy of representation are present. Additionally, the suit must fall into one of three categories. The categories have been labelled by the courts "true," "hybrid," and "spurious." In a "true" action the class members share a common and undivided interest. This means that under law they are recognized as united in interest, as for example, the partners in a limited partnership or a husband and wife in a community property state suing to protect their community interests. In a "hybrid" suit the members share an interest in property, which is the subject of the suit. Their interests are not joint, rather the focus is on the property (typically a limited fund from which they are seeking relief). In a "spurious" action common questions alone authorize the class action. The importance of falling into a particular category is that in effect it determines the binding effect of the judgment. Because of the loose connection existing in spurious suits, courts typically will bind only those class members who opt in to the action. In practice this means that an unsuccessful spurious class suit will bind only the named parties. If a judgment on liability is reached for the class, then the absent members may take advantage of it and enter to seek damages. Judgments in true or hybrid class suits will be binding on all the absent class members.

The most widely used class action statute is the 1966 Federal Rule 23 which governs in the federal courts, as well as in several states. The rule sets out requirements in the first two subdivisions, and then in the remaining three sections provides guidance to the courts on how to manage these actions. These last sections include notice provisions (23(c)(2) and (d)(2)), setting forth when notice is required and what should be included, authority for restructuring the action by subclassing (23(c)(4)), and for allowing absent members to intervene (23(d)(3)), and provisions for approving and controlling settlements (23(e)). The focus is to encourage the development of flexible management devices and to provide the courts with some guidance in that area.

The class requirements under Federal Rule 23 also are stated pragmatically. The party seeking class certification must show that the action meets the requirements set out in 23(a) and falls within one of the three categories of 23(b). The basic requirements in (a) are the same as those just described under the 1938 rule. However, the subdivision (b) categories have been altered to provide more guidance and with the intention that all class action judgments will be binding, regardless of which type of suit is presented. Under Rule 23(b)(1) the focus is on the possible adverse impact of a non-class judgment on the opposing party, who might be placed in an impossible position if faced with conflicting individual judgments, or on the absent class members, whose interests might be practically impaired if class action treatment were denied. Rule 23(b)(2) authorizes class suits in which injunctive or declaratory relief is appropriate on a class basis. Rule 23(b) (3) allows class treatment if common questions predominate and if a class suit is the superior means of handling the controversy.

This last provision is the catchall and there is considerable discretion given to the court to determine superiority. Among other things, the court may take into account whether the action appears to pose severe management problems, what alternatives exist, and whether the suit is important as a policy matter. Because the only connection between the class members in a (b)(3) suit is the presence of common questions, various procedures exist in the other portions of the rule to ensure that their interests are adequately protected. Notice is mandatory in (b)(3) suits and individual notice must be mailed to all identifiable class members, Fed.Rule 23(c)(2). Absent class members may opt-out of the suit and if they do so they will not be bound by the judgment, Fed.Rule 23(c)(3). Conversely, once they opt-out they cannot later take advantage of the judgment. Because these added protections oftentimes are costly and burdensome, it is common to try to fit the action within one of the first two categories so as to avoid these problems.

The final category of class action statutes to be mentioned is just emerging. It is represented by the recently adopted rule in New York, NYCPLR § 10005 (1975), by the newly proposed Uniform Class Action Statute (1976) drafted by the Commissioners on Uniform State Laws and currently adopted in North Dakota, and by various proposed bills being discussed in the Congress. All of these statutes share a common approach—they are long and complex and attempt to deal specifically with most of the many issues that have arisen under the present procedural rules. They provide much more detailed guidance to the courts on how to handle class suits and attempt to provide some solutions to problems about which the courts currently are divided. It remains to be seen whether these new proposals will be adopted more widely, and also how well they will operate.

§ 8–3. Procedural Fairness: Adequacy of Representation, Notice, and Binding Effect

A major problem in the United States in allowing class actions has been how to accord class judgments total binding effect consistent with due process concerns of providing each person an opportunity to be heard. It is absolutely necessary for class judgments to bind even the unnamed members in order to achieve any judicial economy. Thus, the Supreme Court has recognized class judgments as an exception to the traditional rule that only named parties to a suit are bound by a judgment therein. Supreme Tribe of Ben-Hur v. Cauble, 255 U.S. 356 (1921). There will be a failure of due process only when the procedures utilized do not insure the adequate protection of the absent members. Hansberry v. Lee, 311 U.S. 32 (1940).

The two procedures most emphasized to meet due process requirements are an appropriate system for notifying the absent members and a careful inquiry by the court into the named representative's ability to adequately protect those interests. It is not clear whether these requirements are both necessary or if the satisfaction of one may cure a deficiency in the other. The lower courts have split on the question whether some form of notice is constitutionally compelled in all class suits. The Supreme Court's only recent decision in this area rested on a rule interpretation, mandating individual notice in actions under Rule 23(b)(3), but not speaking to actions under the other provisions. Eisen v. Carlisle & Jacquelin, 417 U.S. 156 (1974). Similarly, the Court has not ruled on the question whether actual notice might result in the waiver of a class member's right later to object to inadequate representation. Thus, careful counsel should not overlook either requirement, or the class judgment that is obtained may be subject to collateral attack.

Adequacy of representation is a flexible concept embracing any matter that might influence how vigorously the named party will prosecute or defend the action on behalf of the class. Most central is the question whether the interests of the class and the representative are conflicting or antagonistic. Further, the court may inquire as to the competence of the attorney representing the class or the financial resources of the representatives to make certain that they can pursue the litigation to its end. Because adequacy of representation is so important, the court is obliged to consider that question throughout the course of the suit, not just at the certification stage. However, adequacy problems need not always result in a dismissal. The court can add additional representatives, redefine or subclass the action, or appoint new counsel if that will permit the action to proceed with adequate protection for the absent members.

The basic issue with the notice requirement is whether due process demands some form of actual or individual notice, where feasible, or if alternative constructive or substitute notice schemes may suffice. Further, there is the practical problem of what to include in the notice so as to make it meaningful to the recipient. These issues are now before the courts and to date there is no consensus on them.

§ 8–4. Some Current Problems

A wide variety of problems have surfaced in the class action field. Two of the more important issues will be mentioned here: damage distribution and attorney's fees. One of the biggest difficulties in the damage class suit is how to assess and distribute the remedy when the individual class members' claims are very small or the class is extremely large or it is potentially difficult to identify individual members. A few different approaches have been tried, although all of them are controversial and not widely adopted. In some cases the courts have assessed lump sum damages based on the defendants' records, which reveal illegal profits or overcharges. This alleviates the need for individual damage trials and distribution can be done through a less costly and burdensome method—perhaps even administered by the attorneys. A few courts have gone even further and developed what is called fluid recovery for cases in which it would be extremely costly and probably futile to try to identify class members. Under that approach, after lump sum damages are proven, the court does not attempt to distribute the damages to the class members. Instead, recognizing that class suits are in the public interest, the court devises a means by which the damages can be distributed to benefit the public and yet require little court supervision. For example, in a case in which defendant taxicab company was found to have overcharged, it was ordered to reduce fares for a certain period of time until it had disgorged the improper profits. Daar v. Yellow Cab Co., 433 P.2d 732 (Cal.1967). The Second Circuit has rejected this approach on the ground that it is unauthorized by the rules and violates the defendant's due process right to be confronted by its accusers. Eisen v. Carlisle & Jacquelin, 479 F.2d 1005 (2d Cir. 1973), aff'd on other grounds 417 U.S. 156 (1974).

Another serious source of dispute in the class action field is attorney's fees. Class opponents have argued that class suits are being brought not to vindicate the public interest, but to generate large fees. In many instances this allegation is unfortunately true. Thus, the courts have devoted considerable attention to developing and refining standards for assessing fees in order to keep fees within reasonable limits that will act as an incentive to attorneys, but not result in a windfall profit. The amount of time spent remains the lodestar on which fees are based, although the courts are requiring much more detailed records reflecting the time spent on each aspect of preparation. The novel character and complexity of the case also will be considered. See Lindy Bros. Builders, Inc. v. American Radiator & Std. Sanitary Corp., 540 F.2d 102 (3d Cir. 1974), for a more complete listing of the factors to be considered in setting fees.

B. INTERPLEADER

§ 8-5. History and General Requirements

Interpleader is an equitable device by which a person who admits an obligation (the stakeholder) but is unsure to whom it is owed deposits the money or property with the court and serves notice on the possible claimants that they can dispute ownership among themselves. The action proceeds in two stages. First, the court determines if the use of interpleader is proper. If so, the stakeholder is dismissed from the suit. Second, the court will determine the rights to the property. Those persons served with fair notice and given an opportunity to litigate are bound both against the stakeholder and among themselves. In this way, the procedure acts to reduce multiple litigation and to protect the stakeholder from double or multiple liability or even the threat of it.

Historically, in order to utilize interpleader the stakeholder had to show that he legitimately feared multiple vexation by adverse claimants. The claimants need not be asserting ownership based on the same right, but they had to be claiming exactly the same property. Further, the stakeholder had to allege that he was not independently liable to any of the claimants on some other claims and that he was disinterested in the current stake and did not assert any claim or defense with regard to it. Modern interpleader statutes have largely abandoned these last two requirements and only multiple vexation still need be shown.

Other equitable restrictions may prevent interpleader, however. For example, if the stakeholder has been guilty of laches or contributed to the development of the adverse claims, the court may exercise its discretion to deny the relief. Another limitation that may prevent the use of interpleader

in the state courts is that the Supreme Court has
ruled that an interpleader action is in personam
and that it is necessary for the court to obtain
personal jurisdiction over each of the claimants
in order to bind them to the decree. New York
Life Ins. Co. v. Dunlevy, 241 U.S. 518 (1916).
Most states have not adopted long-arm statutes to
meet this requirement. Thus, interpleader is pre-
dominantly a federal device.

§ 8–6. Federal Statutory and Rule Interpleader Compared

There are two different means of invoking interpleader in the federal courts: one is Fed.Rule
22; the other is by statute, 28 U.S.C.A. § 1335.
Both procedures share some similarities. There
are no requirements that the stakeholder be disinterested or that he not be subject to independent
liability. Under the rule, the stakeholder must
show that he may be subject to "multiple liability." The statute refers to "multiple vexation."
The courts have interpreted both phrases in the
same way so that a showing of the threat of multiple suits will suffice under either provision. Further, the stakeholder may invoke either procedure
on the basis of the possibility of future claims
against the property; he need not wait until claims
have been filed before bringing suit.

Some major differences between rule and statutory interpleader exist. To begin with, different

jurisdiction and venue requirements are applicable to each method. Rule 22 functions like all other joinder rules—actions utilizing it must meet normal jurisdictional requirements. Statutory interpleader has special standards that apply. Thus, in a Rule 22 case, more than $10,000 must be at issue and there must be complete diversity, no claimant may share the same citizenship with the stakeholder. Minimal diversity applies in statutory interpleader—the stakeholder's citizenship is irrelevant. The only concern is that diversity exist between at least two of the claimants. State Farm Fire & Cas. Co. v. Tashire, 386 U.S. 523 (1967). Further, only $500 need be involved. 28 U.S.C.A. § 1335. Personal jurisdiction over the claimants in a Rule 22 case is restricted to that which is authorized under the state law in which the court is sitting. Although Federal Rule 4 authorizes the federal courts to use state long-arm statutes to go outside the borders, most such statutes do not fit the interpleader situation. Thus, a Rule 22 action is territorially restricted—all the claimants must reside in the forum state. Nationwide service of process is available in statutory interpleader. 28 U.S.C.A. § 2361. Finally, venue in Rule 22 actions is proper under the general venue statute where the stakeholder resides, where the cause of action arose (a most difficult place to locate in this context) or where *all* the claimants reside. In actions under the interpleader statute venue may be laid where any claimant resides. 28 U.S.C.A. § 1397.

Two other differences also bear mention. In statutory interpleader actions the stakeholder must deposit the property in issue with the court or post a bond for its value when suit is filed. 28 U.S.C.A. § 1335. There is no deposit requirement under Rule 22, although the court may allow the stakeholder to do so if he so desires. Fed. Rule 67. Thus, in cases in which the stakeholder would prefer to maintain control over the property as long as possible (most commonly so as to be able to use it for investment purposes), Rule 22 interpleader provides the better alternative. On the other hand, the court is given specific authority in the statutory proceedings to enjoin the claimants from suits elsewhere. 28 U.S.C.A. § 2361. Although this injunction power cannot be used indiscriminately to enjoin all related litigation, it does provide a potent weapon to protect the stakeholder from the harassment of multiple suits. The injunctive power of the federal court in actions under Rule 22 is less clear, because the federal anti-injunction statute, 28 U.S.C.A. § 2283, generally prohibits the federal courts from enjoining state proceedings in the absence of specific statutory authority. The only possible applicable exception would be if the court would consider an injunction in this context as "in aid of its jurisdiction." This possibility is by no means certain so that the court's injunction power may be narrower in a Rule 22 action than in a statutory action.

§ 8–7. Assertion of Additional Claims

One troublesome question that has arisen in interpleader suits is whether, once it is clear that interpleader is proper, the claimants may assert additional claims against one another or against the stakeholder. For example, if an automobile insurer interpleads its insured and several persons allegedly harmed by him, can those persons then assert their tort claims against one another in that action? The first thing to note in answering that question, is that any additional claims would need to present independent bases of subject matter and personal jurisdiction. This is particularly so if the claimants are properly before the court only because of the availability of nationwide service of process or minimal diversity. To hold otherwise would create an incredible burden on the claimants and is unjustified by notions of judicial economy alone. Indeed, even if there are no jurisdictional problems regarding the additional claims, it may be questioned whether allowing those claims would unduly complicate or delay the interpleader action and thus whether it is appropriate to inject those new issues into the action. The court will decide that question on a case by case basis.

C. MULTIDISTRICT LITIGATION

§ 8–8. Modern Techniques for Handling

A modern legal phenomenon has been the concept of mass injury. The single act of a nationwide business may affect hundreds or thousands of consumers, a potential securities irregularity may impact on hundreds of thousands of investors, an air crash will injure, often kill, hundreds of passengers. The result of these mass injuries frequently has been the filing of as many lawsuits in courts around the country where the injured parties reside. Thus, considerable attention has been given to ways in which to manage these suits so as to achieve judicial economy while promoting fairness to all concerned.

It is beyond the scope of this Nutshell to inquire in detail into the various techniques that have been utilized. However, two major developments bear mention. The first is the publication of the Manual for Complex Litigation (1977 ed.), written by members of the Judicial Conference and designed to highlight several problem areas in complex litigation and provide some solutions. It contains suggestions regarding scheduling of discovery, discussions of some major issues that have occurred in the class action context, citations to the recent cases dealing with these issues, and many other useful aids for the courts and attorneys involved in those suits.

The second development worth noting is statutory. A 1970 amendment to the Judicial Code established the Judicial Panel on Multidistrict Litigation. See 28 U.S.C.A. § 1407. Comprised of seven judges designated from districts around the country, the Panel is authorized upon application of any party to transfer to one district for coordinated pretrial proceedings all related actions filed in the federal courts. To obtain a transfer the movant must show that the cases share common questions of fact and that transfer will serve the "convenience of parties and witnesses" thereby promoting "the just and efficient conduct" of the actions. By this management device, duplicative discovery and pretrial motion practice is eliminated. Further, the careful selection of the transferee court produces great efficiency by relieving heavily crowded dockets of these cases, as well as assuring the parties relatively prompt action in the transferee court. Under the statute, the actions are to return to their original forums for trial. However, practice to date indicates that most transferee courts retain the cases until judgment is reached or the actions are settled or decided on motion so they never return, thereby further increasing the judicial economies achieved.

IX. OTHER SPECIAL PROBLEMS IN FEDERAL LITIGATION

A. ACCESS BARRIERS

§ 9–1. Standing, Mootness, and Justiciability

The constitutional provision authorizing the establishment of the system of federal courts specifically extends their judicial power only to "cases" or "controversies." Art. III, § 2, U.S. Constitution. Federal courts cannot render purely advisory opinions. The problem of ascertaining what constitutes a valid case or controversy is highly complex and is studied in more detail in courses and books on federal courts or federal jurisdiction. See D. Currie, *Federal Jurisdiction in a Nutshell* 9–28 (1976). A brief introduction follows.

The primary doctrines that have been developed in order to apply the Article III, § 2 requirements are those of standing, mootness, and justiciability. To bring a properly cognizable action in the federal courts, the plaintiff must have standing—the claimant must have suffered a direct or actual injury, as opposed to a more general injury. The presence of an actual injury assures that the questions raised in the suit are not merely hypothetical and that they are being presented in an adversary context comprising a "case."

Further, requiring an actual injury ensures that the plaintiff has a sufficient stake in the outcome that he will pursue the action to the fullest. Plaintiffs aggrieved at public spending cannot file suit against the government solely on the ground that they are taxpayers and are affected thereby. There is no direct injury and standing is not available.

Mootness addresses the same basic question as standing: does the plaintiff have a live or real case. The main difference is the time at which mootness issues are raised. Standing is addressed at the outset of the action. But plaintiff must retain that actual injury throughout the course of the litigation. If he does not, the action is said to be moot and will be dismissed. For example, a prisoner suing to challenge visitation regulations may have standing at the outset. However, if he is paroled or if the regulations are changed before the case reaches judgment, his claim is no longer live and the action may be dismissed for mootness. In this way the federal courts are protected from rendering advisory opinions on hypothetical questions.

Justiciability focuses on the issues being raised, rather than the claimant. An issue may be held non-justiciable because it is not yet ripe for review or because the court feels it involves essentially a political decision, rather than a judicial one. Thus, the concept of justiciability is very fluid. The courts invoke it whenever for some reason they feel that the issues presented in an action should not be decided at this time. The rationale utilized is that those issues do not comprise a controversy of the type envisioned by the drafters of the Constitution.

B. WHAT LAW GOVERNS

§ 9–2. From Erie to Hanna

The question of what law governs in a federal court sitting in a case that is not based on a specific federal law (most commonly, courts sitting in diversity) has posed one of the most difficult problems in federal court litigation. It goes to the heart of the relationship between the federal and state governments. It is a problem studied intensively in advanced courses in conflicts or federal jurisdiction and a more detailed treatment may be found in the Nutshells in those areas.

Until 1938, the balance was tipped in favor of federal control and the federal courts asserted the power to create general federal common law, unless there was a specific state statute on point or the issue was peculiarly "local" in character. This position derived from the Supreme Court's interpretation of the Rules of Decision Act, 28 U.S.C.A. § 1652, in Swift v. Tyson, 16 Pet. 1 (1842). Then, in a series of cases beginning with Erie R. R. Co. v. Tompkins, 304 U.S. 64 (1938), through Hanna v. Plumer, 380 U.S. 460 (1965), the Supreme Court largely returned the power to the states, carefully elucidating the kind of analysis necessary to decide whether federal or state law should govern in a federal court sitting in diversity.

There are two situations that must be distinguished. The first is when the federal court is deciding whether it has the authority to create common law on a particular issue. The second requires the federal court to decide whether it must follow state law even though there is a federal rule of procedure that appears applicable. In the first case, *Erie* makes it clear that federal courts have no power to create a body of general federal common law; that is a power reserved to the states under the Tenth Amendment. The only constitutional interpretation of the Rules of Decision Act is that state law, whether in statutory or common law form, governs on matters substantive. However, when a federal rule is involved we move into an area in which the federal government has a legitimate interest because part of the process of establishing a federal court system as authorized by the United States Constitution (Art. III, § 2) includes prescribing a set of procedural rules to regulate the court system. The question thus becomes whether the rule was properly within the scope of the Rules Enabling Act, 28 U.S.C.A. § 2072. The answer requires an inquiry into whether the rule actually is designed to regulate the processes of the courts or whether it will alter the rules of decision by which the court will adjudicate the merits of the dispute. If the former is so, the statutory and constitutional standards are met and *Hanna* mandates that the federal rule should control.

This description presents the two ends of the spectrum. In many instances the law or issue involved cannot be classified as purely substantive or the federal rule in question may not speak directly to the question involved. A proper analysis to determine whether the federal court is bound to apply state law under these circumstances was suggested in Hanna v. Plumer. It would proceed as follows.

First, ascertain whether there is a federal rule applicable to the issue. If not, then consider the following four factors. One: is the issue one which is tightly or loosely bound up with the creation of the rights being sued upon? Stated alternatively, how substantive is the state's law? Two: would the application of a different rule by the federal court be outcome determinative in the sense that it would produce forum shopping in favor of the federal courts or would result in the unequal administration of the law? For example, different statutes of limitation in federal and state courts on the same causes of action would be very outcome determinative. Guaranty Trust Co. v.

York, 326 U.S. 99 (1945). Three: what is the federal interest in avoiding the state law or the federal policy to be fostered by applying federal law? Four: would the use of a federal standard have an adverse impact on federalism (would it intrude on the state's ability to regulate a legitimate area of state interest)? Byrd v. Blue Ridge Rural Elec. Cooperative, Inc., 356 U.S. 525 (1958). In balancing these four factors, the court in close cases will take into account that the thrust of the *Erie* doctrine is to defer to the states unless some important federal interest is involved or the matter is not one that will interfere with any state interest.

If there is a federal rule that addresses the issue involved, then the second step is to decide whether there is a conflict between the state and federal rules. For example, if the federal rule is discretionary, but the state rule is mandatory, there is no conflict for the court could apply the state law without violating the federal provision. If no conflict exists, then the question is the same as just discussed above—should the federal court be required even to consider the state law—and the same four part balancing test applies. If the federal rule conflicts with the state law, then the federal rule must be found to be properly within the Rules Enabling Act, as described above. If it is proper, the Supremacy Clause, Art. VI, mandates that it control. If it is not within the en-

abling legislation, then the court again is faced
with the four part analysis described above in
order to determine whether it yet must follow
the state law. To date, no federal rule has been
found outside the Rules Enabling Act; therefore,
as a practical matter, once the rules are found to
be in conflict, the federal rule governs. However,
consistent with the general policy underlying *Erie,*
the federal courts will strain to find that the rules
are not in conflict so as to be able to defer to the
state provision when no strong federal interest is
involved.

Throughout this discussion the assumption has
been that the federal court easily can ascertain
the existing state law on a given issue in order
to do the kind of balancing of policies described
above. Unfortunately, this is not always the case.
It is not uncommon for the federal court to be
faced with a situation in which state law is in a
state of flux with no recent ruling by the state
supreme court or in which local rulings may not
exist on the question. In those circumstances the
federal court simply must guess as to the way the
state courts would rule.

§ 9–3. Federal Common Law

The *Erie* case did not remove all authority
from the federal courts to create common law. It
only restricted that power in circumstances in
which the court was sitting in diversity and no

clear federal statutory or constitutional interest pertained so that the Rules of Decision Act mandated that state law govern. The source of authority for the creation of federal common law may be an explicit or implicit statutory grant or, in some instances, it may derive from the Constitution itself. There is no consistent or persistent practice. A few examples should suggest the extent of the federal courts' power.

The most vivid and recent example of a Congressional grant of common law making power is newly enacted Federal Rule of Evidence 501. In that rule the federal courts are instructed to apply to federal cases "the [privilege] rules of the courts of the United States as developed in the light of reason and experience." An implied Congressional directive was found in the labor field when the Supreme Court ruled that when Congress placed special jurisdiction in the federal courts it impliedly authorized them to develop a uniform, national law of collective bargaining, unfettered by what the states might do. Textile Workers Union v. Lincoln Mills, 353 U.S. 448 (1957). Constitutional authority to create common law has been found in the international relations field, Banco Nacional de Cuba v. Sabbatino, 376 U.S. 398 (1964), on questions of apportioning interstate waters, Hinderlinder v. La Plata River Co., 304 U. S. 92 (1938), and in cases defining the obligations of the United States government on federal commercial paper, Clearfield Trust Co. v. U. S., 318 U. S. 363 (1943). The distinction between these latter cases and the *Erie* case itself is one relating to the degree of federal interest. The grant of diversity jurisdiction in Article III, § 2, does not alone establish a federal interest, it merely reflects a desire to provide an impartial forum for out-of-state residents who might feel prejudiced in local fora. When there is a direct federal interest involved, such as those described above, the Tenth Amendment no longer controls and the courts may feel free to create common law in order to implement or protect that interest.

§ 9-4. Federal Law in State Courts

When an action based on a federal statute is brought in the state court, the court is faced with a governing law question for any matter that is not explicitly provided for in the federal statute. Can the state court utilize its own procedures and develop common law on the issue or must it be bound by the approach of law developed in the federal courts? While the statement of the problem appears the same as that confronting the federal diversity court, its resolution is somewhat different. The rationale supporting the *Erie* doctrine was based on the Tenth Amendment's reservation of power to the states. That required the difficult analysis of whether there was some federal interest that would place the case outside the reserve clause. When the action is in state court, however, the Supremacy Clause of the Constitution requires those courts to follow federal law— no careful balancing of interests is necessary.

In order not to place too great a burden on state courts having concurrent jurisdiction, the Supreme Court has ruled that the state may utilize its own procedures for trying the case, as long as those procedures are applied nondiscriminatorily to state and federal cases, Testa v. Katt, 330 U.S. 386 (1947), and as long as they do not impinge on the federal substantive rights being asserted. The state courts are not required to adopt an entirely new superstructure in order to try federal actions.

INDEX

INDEX

INDEX

[257]

INDEX

[*258*]

INDEX

INDEX

INDEX

INDEX

References are to Pages

INDEX

INDEX

INDEX

INDEX

INDEX

[*267*]

INDEX

INDEX

INDEX

INDEX

References are to Pages